Studying Shakespeare

Studying Shakespeare

An Introduction

ANDREW GURR
Professor of English,
University of Reading

Edward Arnold

© Andrew Gurr 1988

First published in Great Britain 1988 by
Edward Arnold (Publishers) Ltd, 41 Bedford Square, London WC1B
  3DQ

Edward Arnold (Australia) Pty Ltd, 80 Waverley Road, Caulfield
  East, Victoria 3145, Australia

Edward Arnold, 3 East Read Street, Baltimore, Maryland 21202,
  USA

British Library Cataloguing in Publication Data

Gurr, Andrew
  Studying Shakespeare: an introduction
  1. Shakespeare, William——Study and
  Teaching
  I. Title
  822.3′3   PR2987

  ISBN 0–7131–6539–1

Text set in 10/11 pt Cheltenham Book
by Colset Private Limited, Singapore
Made and printed in Great Britain
by Richard Clay plc, Bungay, Suffolk

Contents

Preface

This book is meant to be taken, like some varieties of medicine, only after meals. The meals are of course the plays to which the book is addressed. Some digestion of Shakespeare, and in particular the three plays used as exemplary texts, is desirable before you try the medicine. There are of course several different ways of taking these meals. By far the best is experiencing them in the theatre, and that should always be the first choice, so far as it is possible. With modern technology it is also now possible to take the plays in the form of audio cassettes, on film or on video cassettes, and in books. Each of these forms offers a rather different version of Shakespeare, modified not only by the different species of media but through the different sorts of interpretation their producers apply to them, whether consciously or unconsciously. None of the currently available forms offers anything really close to the spoken form for which the plays were originally designed.

For detailed references, the various spoken forms, whether audio or video, are not very convenient. Since words on the page in printed editions offer the most accessible form, quotations in this book are taken from the New Penguin series, and use their act, scene and line reference numbers.

1 Introduction: Why Study Shakespeare?

The study of Shakespeare can last a lifetime. It has absorbed a great many lifetimes already, of course, in the four centuries that his plays have been performed and read. The riches that can come from such study are enormous. It is the purpose of this book to indicate what some of those riches are, and to suggest a few of the better ways of getting at them.

The fact that Shakespeare's plays have been around for four centuries already is to some extent a put-off. They were composed in what amounts to a foreign time, in a foreign language for a foreign audience. And four centuries of readers and performers, while they have clarified some features of the plays, have piled masses of their own interpretations on each play, reading them in ways which are quite as foreign to us as the original texts are. Shakespeare's plays are such a complex mass of words that every age finds it necessary to read them differently. This is right and inevitable. The texts of the plays themselves do not change much, but the readers of the texts do, and so the readings have to be constantly modified by the different kinds of preoccupation each new generation of readers brings to them. The readings of previous generations can easily impede a modern reading. The history of readings of *Henry IV Part 1*, for instance, which is one of the three plays to be used as a test case in this book, tells us a great deal about the interests which each age brought to it. Each age quite rightly reads it in different ways.

Its story concerns a prince, the heir to the English throne. The prince spends his time in taverns with Falstaff, since Falstaff's wit and his company are greatly entertaining. Falstaff wants to draw the prince into breaking the law so that when he becomes king Falstaff himself will be freed from the restraints of law. The question raised early on in the play is when, or indeed whether, the prince will banish Falstaff and the law-lessness for which he stands. In the end (at the conclusion of a second play, *Henry IV Part 2*) he does. Different ages have read this story in different ways. In the seventeenth and eighteenth centuries audiences were hugely entertained by Falstaff, but they felt that the law and the monarchy were vital for social order, and did not question the rightness of the prince's choice in banishing Falstaff. In the course of the eighteenth century, though, monarchy became a much less central feature of government in England. Also, in a society that had become socially and politically stable, human individuality became more interesting and seemed to be more important than social order. Through the course of the nineteenth century, therefore, audience sympathy changed, and began to favour Falstaff over the prince. He came to stand for love of life, and the prince's rejection of him was seen as a victory for repression, for cold political advantage. In the twentieth century, when social order once again became an urgent issue, the balance swung back a little, and the prince became the hero again. He did not, however, regain his status in any straightforward way. Modern commentators refuse to express simple preferences. They see the play as offering a challenging dilemma, for which no one choice can be right except in a very limited perspective. Political advantage says that the prince was right, but the losses in humanity are also considerable. In the twentieth century there are no easy answers, because there are no longer any clear-cut values such as heroism or patriotism or love of life by which conduct like the prince's can be judged.

The lifetime of study available in Shakespeare – and entertainment, and the sophisticated pleasures that entertainment joined with intellectual exercise can give – should proceed step by step through several distinct phases. Each phase has its own distinct rewards. The very first step takes us into the stories as they appear on the stage. For reasons that are set out at length in the second chapter, seeing the plays in performance is the vital preliminary to any further examination of what they offer. Reading the plays privately is not the way to start. They need to be experienced in a group, as part of an assembled audience, for the story as the play tells it. Reading is only a limited and partial means of getting this first excitement. The story in a play has a dynamic of its own. Seeing the play on stage is the best way to discover the shape of the story and to get a sense of its pace. Even a collective classroom or group reading is preferable to reading a script as if it were a novel. A film or television version can make a useful start too. Above all a performance should convey the cumulative development of the play's emotional power.

With the story and its emotional development established, the details of the play can begin to be registered in their places. The intricacies in the personalities of each character, the interplay of relations between the characters, the focus of specific dramatic moments, these can be savoured at leisure. In *1 Henry IV*, for instance, there is a long central scene in which Falstaff and Prince Hal act out in parody their relations and the question whether Falstaff will be banished when the prince becomes king. First Falstaff pretends to be the king and addresses the prince, sadly reproving him for his bad conduct in taverns, but praising the reforming virtues of the knight Sir John Falstaff. Then the prince takes the king's role, and hears Falstaff begging not to be banished. Banish Jack Falstaff, and banish all the world, says Falstaff. The prince replies 'I do, I will'. There is a brief pause, while the audience savours this ominous threat suddenly intruding on the horseplay, before a distraction enters. During the performance there is little time to dwell on this exchange at length. That is a matter for the second step in studying Shakespeare, the more leisurely reading where the implications are analysed. Is the prince suddenly becoming serious and warning Falstaff that he must banish him? Does Falstaff truly recognize what must happen, and are his subsequent struggles to keep the prince entertained self-deceiving? Is the prince's heart really in it? Does he know his own mind, or is the huge delay before he really does banish Falstaff – from the middle of one play to the end of another, altogether seven acts – is that stretch a mark of the prince's inability to come to terms with his duty, which insists that he must banish the world when he becomes king? Most pointedly, perhaps, as we look at this exchange after following the play's story, do we hear the prince's words as the actor spoke them, or do we begin to wonder if they should not be spoken differently? Why does he say firmly 'I do', and then modify it with 'I will'? Is the first merely a part of the play-acting, and the second a promise about the real world? Or is it a change of mind, a postponement of the threat? Our opinion of Prince Hal and our opinion of Falstaff both depend on how we read this exchange.

Equally our opinion of both characters will influence our reading. The story as it runs on stage and the details of the story as we study them on our own will interact as we begin to build up a stronger sense of what is going on behind the story here.

It is chiefly the study of such details in the plays that has absorbed the lifetimes of so many students of Shakespeare. To see the play takes no more than three hours or so. Once seen, or preferably seen more than once, it begins to live in the mind. The details then constantly enlarge and complicate the story, adding to and modifying our sense of the story as a whole. What should then develop is a kind of constant circulation. We have a sense of the play as a whole, which determines how we respond to details like Prince Hal's 'I do, I will'. Each thought, each extra item of information or added touch of understanding about each detail, should slightly modify our view of the whole, and this in turn will modify our view of each detail. A firmly fixed and unchangeable view would be a kind of death, a cutting-off of this circulation.

Usually such a firmly fixed view will apply to the play as a whole rather than to any detail in it. A 'holistic' view of the play, seeing it whole and understanding the parts as they relate to that vision of the whole, is the main target of most criticism of Shakespeare. It has its limitations though. Each published statement about a play, whether published in a book or a newspaper or in a student essay, is rather like spilt blood. It coagulates. The life of a Shakespeare play depends on dialogue and discussion, not fixity. Somehow it is necessary to develop firm opinions, but to keep them circulating, stirred up, mobile, free-flowing, like blood. That is the essential paradox of criticism, and of the study of any literary text. The text is more or less fixed, but the reader is not and never will be, except in death of one form or another. So the reader needs a 'living' critical approach which will respond to the text but keep its liveliness by constantly elaborating and modifying itself. It is an organic process, like growth.

In this book three of Shakespeare's plays are used to demonstrate this circulatory process. It might be said, of course, that the very act of putting details about the circulation of these plays into print is a version of the paradox, since it uses the dead forms of the printed and fixed word to assert the existence of life. That is one version of the paradox of criticism. The technology of communication through books, however, makes it unavoidable. Consequently everything I say should be taken with a grain of salt (although it should also be admitted that salt is normally employed chiefly to give a good taste to dead meat, where no blood is circulating. Metaphors are not always convenient instruments to use when making basic philosophical points). But it is better to work from examples than from abstractions, and the application of the grains of salt is itself a healthy exercise in the process of developing your own ideas about the plays.

The first play to note is the one I have already made some use of, *1 Henry IV*. In a number of ways it is a peculiar case, because it is the second in a sequence of four plays, a sequence which begins with *Richard II* and goes on through *2 Henry IV* to *Henry V*. But *1 Henry IV* has Shakespeare's most celebrated comic character in it, and it stands as an example of one of the two kinds of serious play he wrote throughout the 1590s, a political study based in English history. It was written in 1596. The second example is *King Lear*, written nine years later and widely regarded as the greatest of his tragedies, tragedy being the second the kind of serious play Shakespeare wrote, after he gave up writing plays about English or Roman history. The third example is *Measure for Measure*. This play is a relatively late comedy, written in about 1603 or 1604, some time after the English history plays were composed and after the first great tragedy, *Hamlet*, but shortly before *King Lear*. It lacks some of the verbal exuberance and situational jokes of the earlier comedies, but most of its features are not far removed from them, and it has a wonderfully 'problematic' quality of its own.

1 Henry IV has as its broad subject the questions about kingship which are among the least important of our political preoccupations today. But it has a human element too, which makes the 'foreign' element of the political framework of monarchy a useful frame for some significantly modern preoccupations. It is a play about politicians, figures in authority, who are human beings with human longings. Prince Hal has only a dubious claim to the throne by inheritance from his father, who usurped the title from Richard II. He himself does not, however, suffer directly from the guilt of usurpation which haunts his father, and attention therefore can concentrate more on his personality as a man designated to be the next king than the question of his title to be king, which was the main subject of the earlier history plays. In this sense *1 Henry IV* is about the 'education' of the prince, and the fitness of his personality as a ruler, judge and lawgiver, and the unifier of a nation beset with civil war. He is confronted by two temptations at the outset of the play. The twin characteristics which his father, King Henry IV, calls riot and dishonour are represented in the play by Falstaff, the exemplar of riot and lawlessness, and by Hotspur, the rebellious noble who stands for a simple-minded concept of arrogant chivalric honour, military valour and a different kind of lawlessness. Hotspur's qualities are different from Falstaff's but no less dangerous, signalled by his rebellion against the king. Prince Hal, if he is to prove his worth as a future king, has to defeat Hotspur's lawless honour and at the same time banish Falstaff's lawless riot.

The main focus of interest in the play is necessarily directed at Prince Hal, since everything relates to his struggle against the tempting figures of Falstaff and Hotspur. It seems likely that when Shakespeare started writing the play he expected to be able to show Hal overcoming Hotspur at the battle of Shrewsbury and banishing Falstaff in the same play, at more or less the same moment. Defeating the rebellion by killing Hotspur on the one hand and securing justice by banishing Falstaff on the other were the twin targets set for him by his father's lament about his 'riot and dishonour' at the beginning of the play.

The temptations of Hotspur and Falstaff loom equally prominently for the first three acts of the play, one in the main plot and one in the comic and parodic subplot. But then it seems Shakespeare realized that he had given himself a massive problem if he was to try to get rid of Falstaff as quickly as he could get rid of Hotspur. In these first acts he had made Falstaff too attractive a character to be easily dismissed. So, somewhere near the point where he was writing Hal's 'I do, I will', Shakespeare decided to postpone the banishment of Falstaff to a second play. This meant eliminating Falstaff from most of the last two acts, bringing him back at Shrewsbury to renew the question of his banishment, and then writing a sequel. Consequently in the sequel the priorities were reversed. Where in *1 Henry IV* the main plot was honour and the rebellion and the comic plot was Falstaff and justice, in *2 Henry IV* the main plot becomes Falstaff's riotous behaviour, and the rebellion becomes the sub-plot.

The sequel, *2 Henry IV*, is a masterpiece of structural juggling with that inversion, and also a masterpiece of invented material amplifying the theme of justice, notably with the scenes of Falstaff's misbehaviour in Gloucestershire. But it is equally notable for the almost complete absence of any further scenes of comedy between Hal and Falstaff. Their joking exchanges and Falstaff's seductive antics shrink almost out of sight. The whole sequel is about Falstaff's setting himself up with the illusion that he will not be banished. In the second play Hal and Falstaff never confront each other directly until Hal is king, and at last has to pronounce the formal sentence of banishment on his former 'fool and jester'.

In some sense *1 Henry IV* is therefore a defective play, because the plot is initially set up for a double action whereby the prince overcomes his twin temptations. Halfway through the play this changes so that one of the temptations is not overcome until the conclusion of the sequel, far later than it should be. That postponement of Falstaff's dismissal alters our view of the main focus of attention, Prince Hal. We hear him, after the very first scene of backchat with Falstaff, make the announcement that he knows exactly what he is doing, and is only whiling his time away with his 'base companions' in order to make his eventual reform the more impressive.

> I know you all, and will awhile uphold
> The unyoked humour of your idleness.
> Yet herein will I imitate the sun,
> Who doth permit the base contagious clouds
> To smother up his beauty from the world,
> That when he please again to be himself,
> Being wanted, he may be more wondered at
> By breaking through the foul and ugly mists
> Of vapours that did seem to strangle him.
>
> (I.ii.193-201)

The prince, it seems, is acting on a plan, and for 'a while' will make use of this crew of idlers for the sake of the good publicity their banishment will give him. The trouble is that this cold, calculating knowingness would be more plausible if it led to the banishment rather earlier than it actually does. Is Hal really as cool as this speech indicates, or is he more seduced by Falstaff than he can admit to himself? And in either case, what does this declaration say about the kind of personality which is suitable for authority? It may be necessary for a king to 'banish all the world', but it is certainly dehumanizing. How easy is it for Hal to make such a choice? How two-faced is he about his reasons for his conduct? How honest with himself? What effect does the stretching of the time-scale for his choice have on our assessment of his personality?

Measure for Measure is a play which offers a familiar biblical quotation in its title, and analyses what it means through the story. The title phrase is taken from the Sermon on the Mount in the Gospel according to St Matthew, and refers to the teaching of Jesus about human justice. Traditional interpretations of the phrase in Shakespeare's time saw it as a modification of the laws of the Medes and Persians, which speak of 'An eye for an eye and a tooth for a tooth'. In Christian thinking this revengeful law should be modified by the application of mercy. True justice, or measure as it is called in the play, sets up a story in which a girl is compelled to appeal for mercy to a judge who has condemned her brother to death. The judge then commits the same crime for which he had condemned the girl's brother. The girl, believing he has had her brother executed, is then required, when the judge in turn is condemned by the same law he had used against the brother, to plead for mercy to save his life. The play turns upon the justification for the girl making this plea, which runs against all her own (and anyone else's) natural instincts for revenge.

Shakespeare provides this exemplary analysis of 'measure' and Christian justice by setting up a test case which is based on an extended metaphorical reading of the word 'liberty'. To a great extent *Measure for Measure* is not so much a direct analysis of that complex biblical term 'measure' as a comic extension of the equally ambiguous word 'liberty'. In Shakespeare's time the word chiefly meant what we mean by 'freedom'. In *Julius Caesar* Brutus and the conspirators kill Caesar in the name of 'liberty', because they think that the offer of a crown to him and the reimposition of monarchy in Rome would set up a tyrant who would threaten the traditional freedoms that Romans enjoyed under the republic. At one extreme this 'liberty of the weal' was the tradition of human rights in the commonwealth which human justice and law were supposed to protect. At the other extreme, of course, liberty could mean freedom from any form of restraint, and indeed it could mean complete anarchy.

Law holds the balance between these extremes, serving as what the Duke in the play calls the 'needful bits and curbs to headstrong steeds' (I.iii.20). Shakespeare took a metaphorical application of this range of meanings for liberty, and used it to test the whole question of where the law's middle ground should be. And he applied the term 'liberty' in a very special way. In his time it had one very specific meaning or application: it meant sexual freedom. 'Liberty' was the choice made by libertines, people who believed in total sexual freedom without the legal constraints of marriage. At the beginning of *Measure for Measure* the heroine's brother is put in chains for having, as he bitterly says, 'too much liberty'. His betrothed is pregnant, and he is to be executed because they have not yet completed the legal forms of their love by marriage. In the end the play settles on marriage as the middle ground between complete sexual restraint and complete sexual licence, and thus as a metaphor for the properly merciful rule of law in society generally. Since comedies routinely ended with marriage as a token of re-established social harmony, such a conclusion also helps round the play off as a true Shakespearean comedy.

King Lear is perhaps the most relentless of Shakespeare's tragedies. It is widely regarded as a profound and complex philosophical statement about the nature of man and man's responsibilities in life. Its complexity has led to some radically divergent interpretations of the philosophy, and it is perhaps wiser to think of it as a 'mystery', a metaphysical fable which resists simple moralizing. In a limited sense it can be seen in orthodox Christian terms as a 'mystery' analogous to the crucifixion. King Lear begins prosperous, like the patriarchs of the Old Testament. Like Job he falls into adversity, and is tested by the loss of everything he believed to be valuable at the outset. His beloved youngest daughter, innocent of any evil, the most spiritually rich character in the play, is hanged like a criminal, her death taking away the last piece of property that Lear valued. Cordelia's hanging, a form of crucifixion, poses the same metaphysical questions Christians ask about the crucifixion of Christ. What is man's responsibility for the death of perfect goodness? How do we conceive of a God who permits such annihilation?

The play shows Lear in his egotistical arrogance initiating the sequence of events which gradually strips him of everything, including his sanity, and culminates in the loss of Cordelia. The story is shown in a chain of inexorable causal links from point to point of Lear's descent, and his gradual recognition of his responsibility for it all. The stages of his descent are marked by his own summary declarations about his condition. Once his two elder daughters have stripped him of all material possessions and sent him out into the storm, he says first 'I am a man / More sinned against than sinning' (III.ii.58–9). Later he admits 'I am even / The natural fool of fortune' (IV.vi.191–2). Then it is 'I am a very foolish fond old man' (IV.vii.60). Finally, there is the unanswerable, irreducible truth: 'My poor fool is hanged' (V.iii.303). There is now no more of the egotistical 'I am'. He is nothing, and has nothing left to do but die.

Such a banal summary says nothing about the intensity or the complexity of this fable. The death of Cordelia can affect people intensely. Nahum Tate in the late seventeenth century rewrote the play to give it a happy ending, restoring the original ending from the play that Shakespeare used as his main source. Dr Johnson in the eighteenth century said that he could not bear to see Shakespeare's version of the play on stage because the death of Cordelia gave him such pain. And it was not just pain over the death of a fictional character. To Dr Johnson, as to many generations of Shakespeare students, the relentless clarity of Shakespeare's version of the ending of *King Lear* was a traumatic experience, the plainest presentation of an intense image of life's most painful philosophical question.

These three plays, each in its distinctive way an example of what Shakespeare could do at his best, will provide the illustrations for this introductory visit to Shakespeare territory.

2 Performance Text And Written Text

Shakespeare wrote his plays as the raw material for performance by his own company on his own stage. He had a financial share in his theatre, and very probably helped to design it. He was both an actor in the company and a shareholder in its properties, which included the playbooks, the costumes and their playhouse, the Globe. He knew the stage which was his workshop and the players who acted on it more intimately than any playwrights have ever known the circumstances of performance for their plays. We can be sure, too, that he was not interested in his plays merely being read. We know he wrote altogether at least thirty-seven plays during his working life in London. The only editions of his plays that were published in his lifetime, not more than half of the thirty-seven, came into print either as stolen copies or as versions of the more popular hits released not by the author but by the company, for readers who already knew the plays from their performances. Not until 1623, seven years after his death, did his fellow-players commemorate him by publishing a collected edition of thirty-six of his plays, and so preserved most of what we now think of as Shakespeare for posterity.

Consequently when we read the plays we have to remember that they are play-scripts, not novels or poems. They are raw reminders of Shakespeare's original concept, not the thing itself. Whether we read the plays in modern editions or see modern productions of them, we are experiencing them at a further distance from the form they were designed in than the distance at which we read a nineteenth-century novel or a modern film. Either of these kinds of modern re-enactment, reading or seeing a modern performance, can provide no more than a partial basis for reconstructing the original design. A fully rewarding reconstruction calls for a more active and imaginative participation in the fiction than is required from, say, a realistic novel, where scenes are set by evocative passages of description and human feelings can be conveyed by an observing author who speaks directly to the reader. Shakespeare never speaks in his own voice in his plays, and even his stage directions for the performance are rudimentary. The texts we read are just the remnant scripts, originally intended to be brought to life on the original stage by the original company for which Shakespeare worked. They are only the skeleton, an accidentally preserved relic of the original concept.

That is one view of the play-texts as modern editors have rescued them for us: dry bones assembled in what we hope is the correct shape of the skeleton. The text on the page is still only a skeleton, and organisms cannot live just as skeletons. The appeal which the Chorus makes to the audience in *Henry V* to 'Piece out our imperfections with your thoughts', needs to be answered very positively.

There is also one different view to this about the playscripts, of course. There is no universally agreed truth about Shakespeare. This is the view which treasures the words and the language, and stands in opposition to the view that the texts are only the skeletons of a lost performance. This view refuses to believe that a mind as powerful and versatile as Shakespeare's could possibly have rested content with serving those lucky masses who were idle and free enough to be able to stroll along to the Globe for a few hours' entertainment on a weekday afternoon in 1600. It makes the valid point that there is far more to the plays than any audience could possibly be expected to grasp from a stage performance in the open air on a raw winter afternoon in rainy London.

By this view the playwright must have had in mind a higher, sharper, ideal audience, one which could catch the fleeting allusions to complex political or literary questions, which could dwell on the verbal beauties and ingenuities, and recognize the neat structural parallels and contrasts as part of a design far more intricate and rewarding than the story that is told in the plot. There is an obvious truth in this view. Shakespeare could never have lasted so well through the last four hundred years if he did not have more to offer than what might have satisfied an idle playgoer at the Globe in 1600. He would certainly not be regarded as the world's greatest poet, wordsmith and playwright without it. For most of the last four hundred years he has been read much more often than he has been seen on stage, and indeed we are only now beginning to get enough information about the early theatre to become able to reconstruct the circumstances of his original staging. We ought to start with Shakespeare on the stage. We ought to continue with Shakespeare on the page. Gradually the two different forms of reading will converge on the same central riches.

One thing that reading the plays on the page cannot give is the emotional sweep of the story. Whether or not you know how the story will end, the step by step development of the plot carries with it in a stage performance a growing tension that is intensified by the collective spirit of the watching audience. With books we read at our own pace, stopping when we feel like it and restarting as we please. In a theatre the pace is out of our control. Tension and intensity, the climax and the catastrophe, are controlled by what we witness on the stage. We are in the hands of the actors. To a great extent when we read the speeches from the plays, whoever is supposed to speak them it is always a version of our own voice that we hear. On the stage the actors are separate beings, and we react to them with correspondingly greater intensity as people whom we see doing things and suffering things that are outside our experience. The story lives emotionally on the stage as something to which we are passive witnesses. We share the comic or the tragic resolution with the players, as the climax of a surge of events which has swept us along with the characters. We can never quite do that when we see it on the page, and hear the speeches just in our own voice.

This chapter will look at some of the other ways besides the emotional sweep of the story in which a stage performance can illuminate what the script says. The next chapter will consider some of the ways in which a careful reading of the text (or script) can clarify things that may not be evident on stage.

The main difficulty over the script as performance is the reason why audiences seeing Shakespeare in the theatre over the past three hundred and more years have on the whole had more trouble getting close to the real thing than readers have. Shakespeare in performance is interpreted Shakespeare, someone else's idea of the play. It is not greatly different from reading a book of criticism or interpretation instead of the work itself.

Shakespeare seen in performance today is significantly different from the performances he participated in on the stage of his own time. The theatres themselves have changed their shapes, even more radically than acting and producing styles, which have also changed drastically. There is absolutely nothing wrong with modernized Shakespeare, of course. What it cannot give us is original Shakespeare. And since, on the evidence of the centuries, the original is greater than any of its subsequent interpretations it is worth aiming at a really thorough understanding of the original Shakespeare as it was performed. For that we need to know something of the original theatres and the original staging. This chapter will look at some details of the staging of *Measure for Measure* and the other plays as they were most likely performed by Shakespeare's company.

Measure for Measure was written for staging at the Globe. This chief playhouse of Shakespeare's was an open-air amphitheatre. It was circular, about one hundred feet in outside diameter, and it could crowd three thousand people into a yard in the centre and the three levels of surrounding galleries. The stage was a broad platform jutting out into the middle of the yard, covered by a projecting roof which was supported by two round pillars. At the back of the stage was a wall, the front of the tiring-house or dressing room, with doors in it giving access to the stage and a balcony over the doors. The balcony had several partitions making separate rooms, most of which were used not by actors but by the wealthier members of the audience. The two stage entry doors were positioned below the balcony on each flank, and in between hung a curtain, which when pulled back revealed an alcove or 'discovery space'. The stage platform itself had a large trapdoor in the centre. The distance from front to rear of the platform was nearly thirty feet, or ten yards, and it was nearly fifty feet wide. The players ranged across this large space from the entry doors at the rear, around the two large stage pillars, to the outer edges of the platform where the audience stood.

The audience was arranged very differently from the way modern playhouses place their customers. In the yard and all around the stage, closest to the actors, stood the members of the audience who paid least for their places. These folk were sarcastically called the 'understanders' by the playwrights. They were on their feet throughout the performance, and, in the daylight of the London afternoon when performances always took place, they were wholly visible to the players and to one another. They were the crowd who the players had to satisfy first of all. The slightly wealthier playgoers who did not fancy being on their feet for three hours took places on the benches of the surrounding galleries. They sat behind the crowd who stood in the yard. Those who chose to pay still more had cushions as well as the wood of their benches to sit on. The very wealthiest playgoers had rooms to themselves, the equivalent of boxes in modern theatres. These placed them over the stage behind the players, where they might see less well but where they could certainly be seen, which was probably as important a reason to them for being there as seeing the performance. However poorly they could see the play, they certainly completed the circuit of the audience. It was theatre in the round, the circle of a community of playgoers, with the play at the centre.

The position of the wealthiest playgoers behind the stage should remind us that in this kind of early theatre playgoing was thought to be more a matter of hearing the words than seeing the spectacle. It was not a player's face but his voice and 'action' (the physical movements of acting) that mattered. Beauty certainly did help, though only marginally since all the women's parts had to be played by boys. In any case, there were no stage sets, no scenery and almost no properties which required a view from the front. The stage was bare of anything except easily portable properties such as thrones, beds or banqueting tables and benches. When a scene took place in a throne room or a bedroom the appropriate property signalled the locality – though often enough just one character wearing a crown or a nightcap might convey the same effect. Most scenes required no specific locality. We learn that the opening scene of *Measure for Measure* takes place in Vienna, in the ducal palace, from what the script tells us, not the scenery.

Probably the simplest way to reconstruct the original settings with our imaginations is by visualizing the staging of the four scenes in the first act of *Measure for Measure*. We start with an empty stage platform. Onto it from one of the two flanking entry doors comes the Duke, wearing his ducal robes and crown, and then Escalus and the other members of the ruling council, all properly respectful in manner, keeping their hats in their hands and not turning their backs on their lord.

The Duke makes his first formal speech to them, handing over his administrative powers to Escalus in the presence of the council, and summoning Angelo to take over his duties as chief judge. Escalus mentions immediately (in line 22) that this is Vienna, and announces his approval of the Duke's choice of Angelo. It is a scene of official business, and if we need to think of it as located in a specific place we must imagine it in the council chamber of the Duke's palace. But such localizing is a waste of effort, because nothing beside the clothes and the actions are there to indicate the setting. The characters bring the sense of their localities with them.

In the second scene it is quickly apparent that we are watching a street in Vienna, where Vienna's idle gentlemen stroll and chatter. Its being a public street is made clear when Mistress Overdone and then a captive escorted by guards taking him to prison cross the stage, before Claudio with his party and gaolers also arrive, on the way to prison. All of these groups enter by one of the doors flanking the stage in the tiring-house wall, and leave by the other. The third scene, an exchange between only two characters, is even less localized. Because there is no scenery to be set, each scene follows the other without any pause, and like the quick scene-switching which is so easy in films we jump from one group of characters and their implied locality to another, absorbing the locality from the characters. Only in a few scenes, like the next one in this play, does the actual physical appearance of the stage do any significant service.

In the fourth scene we first meet the heroine, Isabella. She is in the company of a nun, a 'Poor Clare'. The Order of St Clare was the strictest monastic order in the Catholic Church, as an Elizabethan audience would know, and as the nun soon makes clear. Isabella is dressed as a novice, and is evidently eager to join the Order, as she indicates by her comically breathless and worshipful reference to the 'sisterhood, the votarists of Saint Clare'. We might imagine her clasping her hands and looking up to heaven piously as she names the society which she has chosen to imprison herself in. She wishes that their rules might be even stricter than they are. The stage immediately becomes an enclosed place, the secluded nunnery of the Poor Clares. And immediately we hear Lucio calling from '*within*', behind the entry doors, as if he is outside at the nunnery gate. The nun begs Isabella 'turn you the key', to give Lucio access. She and

Isabella are locked into the nunnery, and Lucio is locked out. The nun then leaves by one of the two stage entry doors and Isabella unlocks the other door to admit Lucio, with his air of the Viennese streets from the earlier scene (I.ii). Lucio and his licence have been admitted into the society of the Poor Clares, and by talking to him Isabella is drawn back into association with the world she had wanted to leave. At the end of the scene Lucio leaves by the door Isabella unlocked to let him in by, while she goes out the other door, the one the nun had used, to explain to the Mother Superior what she now has to do back in the outside world. Their separate exits emphasize their different outlooks on life, and the clear preference Isabella has for withdrawal from the sort of 'licentious' life Lucio and her brother are involved in.

In these four scenes the stage platform has been several distinct places, a council chamber, a street, a friar's cell and a nunnery. Only in the last scene was the feeling of an enclosed space important, and there it was emphasized through the by-play with keys and locks in the stage entry doors.

Seeing these scenes on stage, the chief impression would come from the varying numbers of characters involved rather than the varying localities. The Act gradually shifts from groupings of six or more characters to the more intimate scenes between only two characters. The Duke's council with its three speakers and other silent attendants and the street scene with its large groups switches first to the Duke and his priestly confessor, and then to Isabella and the nun, who is soon replaced by Lucio. The scenes with the larger groupings are supposed to take place in the more spacious localities, the scenes with smaller numbers in enclosed spaces. The same actual platform space does for both, because the character groups matter more than the setting. The four scenes of this first Act give us the four groupings we must concentrate on: the people of the Duke's court, the people of Vienna's street life, and then the two chief characters who wish to withdraw from both of these public scenes, the Duke and Isabella. The groupings carry their settings with them.

The other four Acts develop the visual implications of these settings. The Duke, hidden under the monk's gown which is the symbol of his withdrawn life as a 'Duke of dark corners', finds himself drawn into the sexual lives and the prison lives of his transgressing countrymen. From the first discovery that his deputy Angelo is unjust because of his lust for Isabella, through the devices of the 'bed trick' by which Mariana is substituted for Isabella, he learns about the power of sex over human justice. By his efforts to put Barnadine in Claudio's place for execution he learns about imprisonment and the harsher end of the process of justice. And Isabella, dressed at the start as a probationary nun, her equivalent to the Duke's monk's costume, learns too. It is wholly appropriate that the long final scene, in which justice is eventually done by distinctly human and unorthodox means, takes place in the open street. The Duke and Isabella enter for the showdown in V.i in the middle of a bawdy exchange between Lucio and Escalus – 'I think, if you handled her privately, she would sooner confess', says Lucio, and Escalus replies, just as the disguised Duke enters with Isabella. 'I will go darkly to work with her'. Both the Duke and Isabella have by this point learned to abandon their court and nunnery for the human realities of the street. Their protective clothing as priest and nun, finally abandoned as they accept the reality of life in Vienna, symbolizes their urge towards withdrawal from society and the changes which society forces on them both.

Measure for Measure uses clothing as the principal device to underline the main changes which we see the play making in the characters. *King Lear* uses a variety of visible stage properties. In the opening scene Lear indicates how detailed are the material calculations he has done over his 'darker purpose' by waving a piece of paper. The play begins with the courtiers voicing their uncertainty over the king's plans for the succession to his throne. He, by contrast with the first speakers, enters with everything clearly resolved in his mind. First he sends for the King of France and the Duke of Burgundy (l. 33). He gives no reason for this, but it becomes clear as part of his plan when he offers them his unmarried daughter, Cordelia. She is to be married to one of them so that as a married woman with a husband who can rule her inheritance for her she can share the kingdom with her married sisters. The map which Lear takes and flourishes (l. 36) shows how carefully he has planned this scheme. It has marked on it the lines he has drawn to carve up his kingdom, as we see when he tells Goneril, pointing on the map, that her complimentary words have given her all the land 'even from this line to this'. (l. 63). He has calculated his plan carefully enough to give Cordelia the best share – 'A third more opulent than your sisters' (l. 86) – so that he can live more comfortably with her in his retirement. The map provides the clearest possible indication of Lear's secretive and selfish calculations about passing on his material possessions.

Another piece of paper causes more discord in the next scene, when Edmund pretends to conceal a letter from his father in order to make him insist on reading it. Where the map in the first scene indicated Lear's intentions for giving up his property unfairly, Edmund's letter in the second scene seems to indicate his brother's intention of seizing his unfairly. Gloucester takes the evidence of pieces of paper about property in quite as simpleminded a fashion as does King Lear. The piece of paper he waves on stage leads to the banishment of his loyal son precisely as Lear's map led to the banishment of loyal Cordelia. The papers both old men study in these opening scenes indicate their similarity, as men of property closely concerned with and easily fooled over their children's inheritance of their property.

The next stage device appears after the loyal children have been banished, and the loyal servants have confronted the disloyal children. Kent, returned in disguise, is put in the stocks for his attack on a disloyal daughter's steward. Kent is distinctly an old man – Cornwall calls him a 'stubborn ancient knave, you reverend braggart' (II.ii.124). Stocks were a familiar instrument of justice for minor wrongdoers. Putting old Kent in them, and holding him there for a long time – Cornwall says till noon, Regan says overnight – is a mark of how little respect for age authority now has under this new regime. Lear and Gloucester together contrive to have him freed, but Kent's similarity to them in age provides a visual warning on stage of what is to come for them too. He has lost his status, and can easily be victimized. Old age, as Lear later declares, with more truth than he realizes, is unnecessary. Putting Kent in the stocks is a prelude to stripping Lear of his following of knights, and finally banishing him just as he banished Kent. Again, the stage property supplies a visual warning of what is to follow in the story.

King Lear has few other stage properties to display. From here on the story shows the process by which Lear and Gloucester are stripped of everything, on a bare stage. Gloucester loses his earldom and his sight, Lear loses his kingdom and his sanity. Edgar, who is stripped of everything like Lear and Gloucester, symbolizes the process by his changes of clothing. At the outset he is dressed ordinarily. On the heath as Tom a Bedlam he is naked except for a blanket. When he begins the business of helping his blinded father he is given proper clothing again, and at the conclusion he appears dressed for combat. His descent to nakedness, and the climb back again, are visual marks of his changing status.

The only other stage device to give a visual signal is the blood which flows from Gloucester's eyes, and from Edmund when he is wounded in the duel with Edgar. Other characters die offstage by poison or strangling, devices which produce no blood. The stage device which dominates the rest of the play is an audible, not a visual device, the storm and tempest which marks Lear's loss of his sanity. The storm breaks out at II.iv.279, and carries on through most of Act III. Stage directions at III.i.0, III.ii.0, and III.iv.97 and 156 indicate its continuance as an accompaniment to Lear's mad speeches. The storm noises last until the exiles go off into the hovel at the end of this last scene. *King Lear's* storm is one of the most potent examples of the use of atmospheric effects in Shakespeare, a background turmoil which is a constant accompaniment to the words, and a powerful influence on the mood these central scenes generate in an audience. More will be said about the symbolism of what the play calls 'the storm in nature' in a later chapter.

In these three plays the visual indicators which illuminate the stage action are variable, and rarely conspicuous. Taken in isolation they serve chiefly as mute signals, putting emphasis where the words alone are not enough. But strictly speaking, for the sake of the performance text, they have to be taken together with the words. They can only be properly assimilated in their entirety in performance, where they help to shape the audience's emotional response to the play in profound and often unrecognized ways. Usually they indicate thematic parallels or equivalences, such as the link between the solitary Duke and Isabella, or the paper-waving patriarchs Lear and Gloucester. In Shakespeare's staging of his plays such signals are never accidental. The performance as a whole is strongly shaped by the accumulation of many such mute signals.

Besides these individual signals the performance supplies its audience with a good deal more in the way of non-verbal indicators to accompany and shape the text. The effect is usually subliminal in its impact, well below the threshold of an audience's awareness. The rapid succession of scenes, for instance, when a single individual or two characters conferring alternates with large crowd scenes has an effect on a massed audience which solitary reading can never recapture. It generates a pulse of activity, a shift from the intimate and personal to the social and back again, precisely matching the interplay of cause and effect between the individual and society which is a consistent feature of Shakespeare's stories. This interplay between the individual and the social is a major feature of history plays like *1 Henry IV,* and of comedies like *Measure for Measure.* In *King Lear* that consistent pulse develops a striking new rhythm, as the large social group of the opening scene breaks up into smaller units. Kent and Edmund stand out as solitary plotters, for their different purposes. The exiled Lear and his shrinking entourage clash with the court servants of Regan and Goneril, before they join up with the followers of Cordelia. The society visibly breaks apart, shifting and regrouping, forced to go alone like Edgar or to make new social and antisocial unions like Edmund. The final scene offers a renewed social unity in desolation, as the obtuse Albany in the final scene, slowly fumbling his way towards comprehension of what has been going on, tries vainly to re-impose order and authority on the chaos Lear has generated.

3 Structure: Narrative and Poem

A play has some of the properties of a novel. It has a story to tell, and tells it in the sequence and with the techniques that a novel normally uses. It alternates between one group of characters and another, keeping different threads of the story going, entwining the lines of main plot and subplot in a complex sequence from the exposition to the resolution. That is the way the full story of a novel is usually set out, the different strands creating a pattern of parallels and contrasts around the central theme.

Most plays, and especially Shakespeare's, have all these narrative characteristics, but they also have the properties of a poem. They use language to weave verbal chains which create an imagistic structure. If you think of them in this way, *King Lear* can be read as a hugely elaborate poem about the meaning of 'nature'. *Measure for Measure* then becomes a teasing-out of the complex ambiguities inherent in the word 'liberty'. *1 Henry IV* generates an image of Prince Hal crowned with the two shameful garlands of riot and dishonour, and shows how he behaves before displacing such unkingly crowns with the proper royal crown.

Drama, possessing as it does both the narrative properties of prose fiction and the imagistic properties of poetry, needs to be approached with a critical apparatus that can master each kind of property. The kind of criticism appropriate to novels can be applied to Shakespeare, but will neglect the plays' poetic strengths. Similarly, the kind of criticism appropriate to poetry is bound, when applied to Shakespeare, to neglect the wonderfully strong and subtle narrative qualities in the plays.

It will be the job of the two chapters following this one to discuss first the narrative properties of the three plays which are the exemplars in this study, and then their poetic properties. In this chapter it is necessary to begin by tackling the problems which develop when we combine the two into what is sometimes called the 'holistic' approach. In the process, for reasons which will become clear shortly, this chapter will also consider the features of the plays which become available more readily through a solitary reading of them than through enjoying a performance on stage.

The 'holistic' approach to Shakespearean drama is something that has to a large extent been generated by the placing of the plays in the centre of examination syllabuses. Concern for the 'themes' of the plays, the need to summarize what general subjects they are concerned with, the immediate question of what they are thought to be about, these are all examination attitudes. They reflect the examiners' need to persuade students to write their idea of a play down on paper in half an hour, a page or a sentence, with the kind of summary statement that indicates how fully (whatever that means) the student has 'understood' (whatever that means) the text assigned for the examination. You cannot readily do that without a sense of what the whole play is 'about'.

The trouble with such an aim is that it is bound to lead to vast oversimplifications if not to distortions of the text. A summary statement of what a play is 'about' automatically excludes from consideration all the features, or the range of other possible features, which are not accepted in the summary statement. If you say that *King Lear* is about the proper relations of parents and children, you cannot easily say as well that it is about authority, or that it is about the morality of nature, or that it is about the Christian concept of adversity, or that it is about human attitudes to divinity. And yet the play is about all of these things, and many other things besides.

Every reader needs to develop a sense of what the play is about, just as every member of an audience develops a similar sense (less voluntarily, less individually, because of the collective feeling each performance generates, and because each stage production is already trying to be a directors' and actors' interpretation of what the play is about). This developing sense of what the play is about is one of the first standard devices our minds bring to bear on any new experience, and especially any new fiction. We are always trying to make sense of our experiences, and we usually begin to do so by reducing them to a simple pattern, something familiar and recognizable. That is a necessary preliminary before we can begin to acknowledge the dissimilarities, the new and uncomfortable angles, and start the next step, which involves fitting them into the old pattern so that the old pattern is slightly modified, or making a new pattern. Most formulations of what a play is about are patterns that have already become familiar from other experience.

Everybody's patterns are different, because everybody's experience is different. There are always similarities in the patterns though. Human communication would be impossible without a shared body of experience. Language itself is a shared experience, and communicates new experiences as it communicates new words, through the use of older and therefore familiar forms. By extension literature does the same. It offers an author's own pattern for his or her experience, and sets it up for others to recognize. The great myths and the great literature of any culture are a form of language, making closer communication and exchange of new experience possible by their analogy, however remote, to the familiar standard myths. The importance of the function of the individual reading of the plays of Shakespeare is to a large extent that it supplies a means of accommodating personal and individual experience, necessarily unique, to the distinct version of familiar myths expressed in the plays. A personal pattern of experience is set against and modified by the patterns seen in the plays.

The value of reading the plays is a double one. On the one hand it offers the opportunity for close analytical study of particular 'cruxes' or moments of significant paradox and doubt. And on the other it offers the opportunity for a wholly individual response to the story, both as a whole and in all its details. The character of Isabella in *Measure for Measure*, for instance, is one which evokes a wide variety of responses. In the story as a whole she changes drastically, from the young innocent eager to escape from life into the convent, to an honourable trickster, and finally into a woman who learns to suppress her own instinct for revenge so that she can plead for mercy to be given to the man who has injured her. Her last choice, whether or not to accept the Duke's offer of marriage, is finely balanced, and different productions on stage have treated it very differently. She can marry the Duke who has taught her the quality of mercy. She can spurn the Duke who has tricked her. Or she can marry him in gratitude for saving her brother's life. On stage only one version of this conclusion is possible. On the page a reader can choose more freely, and more in accordance with the personal pressures generated by the individual response to the text.

In different ways both of these advantages which come from the reading of plays work against a holistic view. A particular ambiguity or paradox and a variable preference over the resolution of the story both inhibit any easy generalizations. The real value of a holistic idea about a play lies in what help it can give in the process of what we sometimes call 'making sense' of an experience. The isolated ambiguity or paradox is pointless without a context, a sense of the whole play to which it relates. In *King Lear* IV.vi one of Cordelia's gentlemen tells the mad Lear 'Thou hast one daughter/Who redeems nature from the general curse/Which twain have brought her to.' This can mean that Cordelia is the daughter who will rescue Lear from the curse of Goneril and Regan, but it also echoes the biblical idea of Christ who redeems all human nature from the curse of original sin. It has a further connotation in the play too, since it makes nature into Dame Nature, afflicted by 'her' general curse, which is not just original sin but the human nature set up as his god by the villainous Edmund in the second scene of the play. None of these resonant words would make much sense if they could not be related to the larger patterns in the play, where Cordelia becomes a redeemer figure who like Christ has to be sacrificed, and the other two daughters with their lechery and their materialistic callousness become emblems of the worst in human nature.

The other side of this process is also part of the holistic approach. The larger issues in *Measure for Measure* are strengthened and clarified as we come to terms with the changes in Isabella, and reach our own complex conclusions about her final choice. The murder of Cordelia by hanging in *King Lear* will not develop the associations with the crucifixion if we do not register the implications of the anonymous gentleman calling Cordelia a redeemer, and the whole intricate pattern of conflicting references to nature will be merely confusing without a sense of the variety of ways in which different characters use the word. That is the basic function of the holistic approach.

Individual readings of a play can operate best when they

inhibit the looser kinds of holistic interpretation. In some degree any stage production is a holistic reading, and a necessarily oversimplified one. An individual reading can correct that tendency. The very first lines spoken in *1 Henry IV*, for instance, are a seemingly straightforward statement by the king of his worries: 'So shaken as we are, so wan with care, / Find we a time for frighted peace to pant. . .'. All actors speaking these lines, and indeed most editors and commentators, have assumed that here Henry IV, the man who in the previous play usurped the throne of Richard II and took his crown, is expressing his tormenting guilt over his crime. He uses the royal 'we' to express his personal unhappiness. Throughout the play the king is unhappy, and in the following play he openly admits the torment of guilt over his act of usurpation. Actors always stress his guilt, starting with this opening speech.

Readers of the text, however, can soon find reasons to be more cautious. The king in these lines is celebrating the end of the rebellion which followed his seizure of the crown, and declaring that he will lead a crusade to the Holy Land. At the end of *Richard II* he had declared that he would go to Jerusalem to expiate Richard's murder, but on a pilgrimage of guilt, not a warlike crusade. This change of plan means that he will now lead his army out in an honourable Christian fight against the heathen. He has exchanged the idea of an act of solitary penitence for a collective act of grace joined with his fellow-countrymen. The war at home has been won, the war of grace abroad can now begin. The care and worry caused by the recent civil war, however, calls for a rest before the crusade begins. That is what he is announcing at the beginning of the play. The crusade will then unite the fighting elements in the country again, against their common enemy. The 'we' of these opening lines is the king and all his followers together. They are all shaken and wan with care. The point that they are collectively wan is made clear in the conclusion of the speech (lines 28-31), when the king switches from the collective 'we' to the personal 'me': 'But this our purpose now is twelve month old, / And bootless 'tis to tell you we will go. / Therefore we meet not now. Then let me hear / Of you, my gentle cousin Westmorland . . .'

The problem which an actor has with these lines is that he can only deliver them in one way. The reader can read them in several ways, and compare the value of one with another. On stage the actor of the king usually stands apart, addressing his nobles from the distance of his private guilt. That of course is one likely reading of the lines, and the one all commentators have accepted, given the context supplied by *Richard II* and the worries which the king expresses throughout the two *Henry IV* plays. It also conforms to the usual manner of royal speech in which the ruler speaks of himself in the impersonal plural. But it is less vivid than a reading which makes the king here try to reassure his nobles, to make common cause with them and to encourage them to support his decision that they should all go together to Jerusalem on a crusade instead of the king going alone on a guilty pilgrimage. He wants unity, so he uses the collective form of address between equals, not the more distant royal form. It is a not untypical Shakespearean tactic that this distinct variant of the usual royal form of address only becomes apparent thirty lines further on. The presence of this particular group of nobles with whom he expresses common cause in this scene becomes important later. Westmorland is a kinsman, Sir Walter Blount gives his life for Henry at the battle of Shrewsbury which ends the play. The supporters who helped him to the throne in *Richard II* are absent, not yet the rebels they become by the end of the first act, but not the loyal followers Henry needs to take with him to the Holy Land. The reader can easily savour the possibilities of such a reading while setting it against the standard, more conventional reading. On stage it can only be taken one way.

4 Narrative Qualities

No Shakespeare play tells a single story. In *1 Henry IV* there is a main plot in verse, the story of the king and prince facing rebellion and its hero Hotspur, and there is the sub-plot, the prince with Falstaff and his seductions. Traditionally the sub-plot was in comic prose, often burlesquing the events and characters of the main plot. That is one function of the Falstaff scenes in *1 Henry IV*, with the prince's parody of Hotspur and his manner and the game played between Hal and Falstaff mimicking the king's instructions to his heir over his riotous companion Falstaff. Falstaff's catechism about honour reflects comically on Hotspur's exuberant speech about plucking bright honour from the pale-faced moon (I.iii.199-205). *King Lear* also has a sub-plot, though not a comic one. The story of Gloucester and his children echoes and forms contrasts with Lear's. Lear is an active, commanding figure, defying the elements and the consequences of his own actions. Gloucester is a passive figure, ascribing all wrong to the arbitrary whim of the gods, fatalistic, and so despairing when adversity strikes him. His experiences match Lear's while his different philosophy takes him along a different path. Events destroy Lear's controlling reason and leave him mad. They destroy the impercipient Gloucester's eyes and leave him blind. In both plays the two main stories interlace their various threads and offer varying patterns of comparison and contrast.

Measure for Measure is rather differently constructed. It is a feature of all Shakespeare's comedies that the web of their story-lines is more intricate and more consistently interwoven than the plots in the 'serious' plays. There is no recognizably distinct main plot and sub-plot. Any separation in the stories to which the different characters belong is rather a matter of social rank than of parallel but unconnected events. *Measure for Measure*, being about sex and marriage, provides a range of characters all of whom are struggling with the same problem, and whose resolutions of the struggle vary only in degree, a degree which relates closely to their social status. The scenes with Mistress Overdone and Pompey are more clownish than the scenes between the Duke, Isabella and Angelo, but they do not function as burlesques of the central subject. They are equally concerned with the relationship between sex and the law. Their comedy simply fits the lowest social and philosophical point on the scale of possible attitudes.

It is necessary to start with the different threads of story because the focus of a 'holistic' view of each play largely depends on what is thrown up by the pattern of parallels and contrasts. The central subject of each play is the unspoken issue that lies between the various parallels. At the beginning of *1 Henry IV*, for instance, the riot and dishonour that crown Prince Hal are contrasted with the honour that attends on 'the gallant Hotspur', 'the theme of honour's tongue', as the king calls him. The Prince and Hotspur never meet until their duel at Shrewsbury in the final scene of the play, but all through there lies between them the question of the real nature of honour, and particularly the concept of honour appropriate to a prince and ruler.

It is best to begin by looking at the narrative structure of *1 Henry IV* first, because its pattern is the simplest of the three. The twin stories of honour (in the main plot) and riot (in the Falstaff plot) run in alternate scenes through the first three acts of the play, before the decision to postpone Falstaff's banishment forced some adjustments and largely set the sub-plot aside. The first three acts are entirely characteristic of Shakespeare's standard technique for exposition of his stories.

Shakespeare always followed a five-act pattern for his plays. The first act sets up the situation which the second act develops, leading to a third-act crisis. This is followed by some regrouping in the fourth act, beginning the build-up to the catastrophe or resolution in the final act. *1 Henry IV* opens with a discussion between the king and his loyal cousin which 'places' the action. The rebellion following Richard II's deposition has been crushed, thanks in large part to Harry Hotspur's exploits, which the king contrasts sadly with the dissolute behaviour of his own Harry. The second scene immediately gives us the dissolute Harry, and his plan to use the rioters as clouds through which he will shine in greater glory when the time comes. The third scene launches Hotspur's rebellion. This is the situation to be resolved in the battle at Shrewsbury which forms the plays's finale.

The parallels in this first act are not conspicuous, but they are quite distinct. Hotspur plans rebellion, and glories in the battles in prospect. Prince Hal plans to share in the robbery at Gadshill, an inglorious game of disguise and trickery which will foil the robbers but bring no honour of the sort Hotspur pursues. Hotspur is disloyal to his king, Hal apparently disloyal to the law, both for their own ends.

The second act begins with the carriers who are to be robbed, and their betrayers. The scene between the pickpurse Gadshill and the chamberlain at the inn is often cut from performances, but it is important for the way it identifies the robbery as more than just Falstaff's game. The chamberlain makes his living by spying on travellers and informing the pickpurses. Thieves are not the less thievish for being fat and playing the fool. This background for Falstaff also reflects on Hotspur, who enters after the fiasco of the Gadshill robbery speaking of his fellow-rebels in exactly the tone and the terms Falstaff has just been using of Hal and Poins. He treats his wife Kate in exactly the same comic fashion as Petruchio does his Kate in *The Taming of the Shrew,* but with very much more serious matters at issue. The urgency of Hotspur's affairs in its turn reflects on Prince Hal's carefree attitude of casual relaxation which follows when he makes fun of Francis the drawer. He makes the point himself when he says 'I am not yet of Percy's mind, he that kills me some six or seven dozen of Scots at a breakfast', and mocks his relationship with his wife. Falstaff accusing him of cowardice at Gadshill underlines this point. 'You, Prince of Wales!' says Falstaff bitterly, thinking not of riot but of dishonour in this inverted setting for military valour. After the game with his own cowardice has been played through, he repeats the point.

Thou being heir apparent, could the world pick thee out three such enemies again, as that fiend Douglas, that spirit Percy, and that devil Glendower? Art thou not horribly afraid? Doth not thy blood thrill at it?

The final part of this last scene in Act II shifts the focus back from honour to riot, in the double playacting of the scene between the prince and his father, and the prince's promise that he will indeed banish Falstaff. The act nonetheless ends with the prince protecting his jester by sending away the officers of justice.

The third act's climax is the confrontation between the king and the prince. Framed on the one side by the rebels and their own discord, and on the other by Falstaff and confirmation that the prince has repaid the money taken at Gadshill, this scene draws all the threads together. Indeed, it draws on threads from the earlier play, *Richard II*, and looks forward to *Henry V* as well. The king emphasizes how much he owed to 'opinion' in usurping the crown from Richard, and how much Prince Hal now looks like the Richard who lost his crown. Public opinion becomes a major political consideration when Falstaff is known to be the prince's companion, and especially when he has not yet given any theme for honour's tongue to redeem him. The prince's reply is first that he will be more 'himself', and secondly that he will acquire Hotspur's honours by defeating him. In his reply to his father he gives no sign of intending to banish Falstaff, only that 'I shall make this northern youth exchange / His glorious deeds for my indignities.' From here on the question of the prince's honour becomes the central issue, and riot quietly moves aside.

Act IV is entirely given over to the manoeuvres before the battle. The rebels are divided, the king's forces firm. At the beginning of Act V the king's offer of a peaceful resolution to their differences is lost among the divided forces of the rebels, and the outcome begins to depend more and more heavily on the morale-boosting effects Hotspur's valour has on the rebel forces. Prince Hal, in Falstaff's company most of the time, now stands in utter contrast to him, his valour set against Falstaff's discretion. Falstaff has to remain in view, but the question of the prince's indulgence in riot is now irrelevant because the focus is on the military virtues. The king acknowledges that Hal has 'redeemed thy lost opinion' (V.iv.47) in valour and loyalty even before he kills Hotspur. Falstaff's snatching of the corpse and Hal's honour serves only as a reminder that the prince has more redeeming still to do.

The two plots of *King Lear* progress along similarly inter-twined but largely separate lines. The two stories are closely linked by parallels of character and situation. The loyal and banished Edgar and Cordelia are balanced against the bastard

Edmund and the 'pelican daughters'. The blinded Gloucester is pushed out of his home like the mad Lear. These equivalences are matched by the use of the same words for both stories. Edmund is a 'loyal and natural boy' until his ingratitude is known, when he becomes the same as Lear's 'unnatural daughters'. Cordelia can say 'nothing' to Lear's demands, and Edmund pretends that the forged letter from Edgar contains the same dangerous 'nothing'. The language of *King Lear* has the tightest weave of any of Shakespeare's plays.

In *1 Henry IV* the two plots dealt with very different qualities, riot and dishonour. The closeness of the parallel plots in *King Lear* makes the pattern of equivalences more delicate, and calls attention more to the contrasts than the similarities. Gloucester's good will and his passive fatalism emphasize by contrast the violent unreasonableness of Lear's conduct. Equally the bestial selfishness of Edmund ('Now gods stand up for bastards!') prepares us for the lechery and the self-interested plotting of Goneril and Regan. In the conclusion the news that Gloucester's heart 'burst smilingly' when he rediscovered his banished son looks back to the reconciliation of Lear with Cordelia, and intensifies the contrast of his death while trying to confront the fact of her murder.

The narrative structure of *King Lear* follows the five-act pattern fairly loosely, because its events flow without pause or digression. From the initial two scenes in which first Lear banishes Cordelia and then Gloucester is duped over Edgar the action moves relentlessly on to the climax in the storm and tempest of Act III, where Lear and Gloucester are stripped of everything, including reason and eyesight. The final scene is a lengthy series of reversals of expectation set up chiefly by the contrast between the Gloucester story and Lear's story. Gloucester's happy death and the victory of Edgar in combat with his brother might lead us to expect the same ending that we are given in the old *King Leir*, a play which Shakespeare may have acted in, and which he used as one source for his version. In the old play Leir and his daughter survive to live happily ever after. In Shakespeare's play Edgar's victory seems to prepare the audience for a parallel victory in the main plot, as anyone who remembered the old play would expect. The entry of Lear with Cordelia dead in his arms nullifies that parallel. Albany then makes two attempts to restore a form of order. First he declares that he will resign his authority as the sole remaining son-in-law and give the kingdom back to Lear, while making sure that rewards and punishments are handed out fairly: 'All friends shall taste / The wages of their virtue, and all foes / The cup of their deserving.' But Lear checks that idea with the unanswerable point that justice cannot be done, because 'my poor fool is hanged'. Cordelia's murder makes a nonsense of any attempt to impose earthly justice. After Lear dies Albany tries again. Ignoring that fact that it was the division of the kingdoms that launched the whole sad story, he turns to Kent and Edgar and asks them to take over from him, exactly as Lear had done with Cornwall and Albany in the opening scene. Mercifully, before the wheel of the main plot can come full circle as Edmund has just said his plot has, Kent declines the offer. Edgar survives on the wheel of the Gloucester plot. Nobody survives from Lear's family. The ending is a pattern of precise and unpredictable contrasts.

Measure for Measure is based on the gamut of human attitudes to sex and the law. The issue is 'government', as the Duke says in the opening lines of the play, and specifically the government of human sexual urges. There are four marriages at the end of the play, each serving as the conclusion to its own story of 'liberty'. The Duke and Isabella, Angelo and Mariana, Claudio and Juliet, with Lucio and his punk emerging from the world of Mistress Overdone, make four intertwined stories. They occupy a gamut of social positions ranging from a distinct preference for the law over liberty at the top end, to an equally distinct preference for liberty over the law at the other. Between them they provide the play with four plots. The story of the Duke and Isabella is a development from the love of solitude and moral rigour to engagement with human frailty. The two central marriages present alternative attitudes to the complex business of Elizabethan marriage. Traditionally, marriages were settled by the troth-plighting, whether it was agreed between the two lovers or (more often) negotiated by their parents. Usually some complex financial negotiations followed before the formal legal and church ceremonies which completed the accord. Sex between the two might take place at any stage between the troth-plighting and the church. Claudio and Juliet started early. Angelo was slower, and coldly decided to break off the engagement on financial grounds, after the initial plighting which gave Claudio and Juliet their licence. One marriage was evidently impelled along by sex, the other blocked by money.

There are in fact more than these four main strands to the plot, since the fate of Mistress Overdone and her bawdy house is separate from Lucio's story, Barnardine's fate also enters into question, and the lines of the Duke and Isabella converge only very gradually through the course of the play. But they are all interrelated either directly, as with Isabella and Claudio, or by the parallelism of their situations.

The first act makes it difficult from the start to separate the various strands. The Duke broaches the question of law-enforcement in his two scenes, and sets up the situation as a test for Angelo. It is not until the end that we are to realize it has also become a test for the Duke. Claudio's imprisonment in the second scene shows one immediate consequence of the Duke's decision, and that brings in Isabella. The parallel between the Duke's fourteen-year withdrawal from society, which has brought about the lax enforcement of the law, and Isabella's desire to submit herself to the strict restraints of the Order of St Clare is not emphasized at this point.

The second act shows the enforcement of law, Angelo's failure as judge, and Isabella's agonizing choice between her brother's life and her own virtue. By now it is clear that there is only the one plot, in which all the characters are trapped equally, and death is the hazard at the end of the trap. The presence of the disguised Duke is the only hope of rescue. His entry to begin the third act, still disguised as a friar, immediately after Isabella has been confronted with her choice, underlines that point. He will have to intervene. Consequently the great speech he makes to Claudio at the beginning of the act, 'Be absolute for death', must sound daunting. The Duke is maintaining the principle for which he pretended to leave Vienna, to allow the law to be re-imposed in all its severity. But when Isabella arrives at the end of the Duke's speech and the Duke then overhears the exchange between Isabella and her brother, the plot's development makes nonsense of his absolutism. It follows naturally that he should promptly set up the bed trick as a device to foil Angelo.

As Act II was largely Isabella's, in her two confrontations with Angelo, so Act III is the Duke's. Having met Isabella and her impossible choice, and having been drawn by it into plotting to evade the letter of the law, his superior position is undermined further by his exchange with Lucio. The Duke of dark corners is learning a lot about his subjects from his eavesdropping. At the end of the act he sums up his conclusions by speaking those curious doggerel rhymes which elaborate the biblical point 'judge not lest ye be judged'. Together these two acts take the single story forward, transferring the choice and the responsibility from Isabella to the Duke, and entangling them both in the social struggles that both originally wished to retire from.

The fourth act sets everything up for the Duke's return to the streets of Vienna at the beginning of the fifth act, and his enforcement of the justice which he has seen so dismally misused. He stage-manages things so that Isabella suffers first, having to expose her 'shame' in the public street, and being spurned. His own exposure comes next, when his disguise subjects him to his own law, so that, as the cogent stage direction puts it, *'The Provost lays hands on the Duke'*. He then sets up the real test for Isabella, the reason why he kept from her the news that her brother is not dead as she believes. She is made to plead for Angelo's life as an act of Christian mercy, against all her own instinct for justice and revenge and a literal interpretation of the 'measure for measure' tag. Angelo's 'act did not o'ertake his bad intent'. He should therefore not be punished as Claudio, who actually did his deed, was punished.

And so the Duke moves back into his judicial role to issue his rewards and punishments. Barnardine is pardoned, and put into the friar's care. Claudio is pardoned for Isabella's sake. That pardon ensures Angelo's pardon too, since he can now be seen to have committed no crime either on Claudio or on Isabella. Lucio's punishment is marriage to the woman who bore his child, and then whipping and hanging, though the latter two punishments are promptly remitted. There remains only the Duke's marriage to Isabella, though characteristically the embarrassed Duke has to have two goes at proposing, and equally characteristically the idea leaves Isabella mute.

The gamut of attitudes to sex, and the prospective marriages that provide a uniform close for each attitude, remain the same throughout the play. The only uncertainty is over how the various resolutions are to be made. In the plot the real progress is the way in which the two figures at the law-inclined end of the gamut come to learn that the law on its own is not enough. From a position of seclusion at the start they are both made to question their own positions, and to engage in social machinations which are a world away from their initial preferences. The Duke's proposal to Isabella does come as something of a surprise, and the shock is a nudge to the audience about the distance the central characters and their attitude to the central issue have travelled.

This summary of the narrative structures of the three plays used as examples in this book is necessarily far too condensed. It makes little mention of the way one scene is juxtaposed with another to illuminate both through the pattern of parallels and contrasts. It makes no mention at all of the way in which the different threads of the story are held together, or the way in which the accumulation of scenes gradually builds up an expectation in the audience, that mixture of confident expectation and surprise which makes the resolution both exciting and right at the same time. Shakespeare was a master of dramatic structure and a matter of exposition. It is not possible to pick out more than a few of the many features which show this mastery.

5   Poetic Qualities

Words are fluid. Their meanings, denotation as well as connotation, alter according to the circumstances in which they are used. This fluidity is restricted a little when only one person uses them, and it is restricted much further when they are locked into a fixed set of circumstances such as a literary text. The games which are played with words such as 'honour' in *1 Henry IV*, 'liberty' in *Measure for Measure* and 'nature' in *King Lear* intensify and settle the definition of each word for the purposes of the play itself. Some words may be enhanced more generally, as with the phrase used for the title of *Measure for Measure*. The complete play provides a full linguistic and social context for each word used in it.

When a wordsmith as dexterous as Shakespeare uses language in a play, however, the words do not congeal or become less dynamic for being fixed in a context. The same word will shift its meaning depending on where and when it is used, and by whom. 'Honour' means something quite different to Hotspur from what it means to Prince Hal or Falstaff. The word 'nothing' with which Cordelia answers Lear's demand to express her love for him, and which Edmund uses to excite his father's curiosity over the contents of his piece of paper, have only a marginal connection in relating the two good children to each other. But the word is also used to point up a significant difference in outlook between Lear and his good daughter. Lear's thinking is materialistic. At the outset he is an Old Testament patriarch, proud like Job of his riches, preoccupied with carving up his possessions and settling the best of them on Cordelia so that he can live comfortably with her in his retirement. She thinks the opposite way, in New Testament terms. Spiritual riches go with material poverty. The point is underlined when her two suitors are invited to take her without any dowry. Burgundy cannot accept such a bargain, but France says she is herself a dowry, and takes her for her virtue, not her inheritance. She is, as he says, most rich being poor.

Lear's ignorance of the spiritual point that lies behind that paradox is shown in his reaction to her first answer, that she can say nothing. 'Nothing will come of nothing' was an old tag from Lucretius, the Roman materialist philosopher. Christian dogma would argue that, despite Lucretius and the materialists, Christ came of nothing, by virgin birth. And his existence made redemption for humankind possible. The comment in Act IV that Cordelia redeems human nature from the general curse is made when Lear has been stripped of all his material possessions, and has only Cordelia's love to rescue him. The word 'nothing' thus becomes resonant with Christian significances, and draws attention to the first of the many paradoxes that rule the use of words in *King Lear*.

In examining the web of words which make every Shakespeare play, *King Lear* must be the prime example. Its web is so tightly meshed that each recurrence of a key word shifts its meaning slightly, and adds more resonance to it. The whole play seems to be constructed upon a few key words, which flex and expand as they are deployed in different contexts until they seem to comprehend the whole paradoxical structure of the story. Pressure is applied to such basic concepts as 'nature', 'reason', 'justice', and each is put through the shredding process which all orthodox and firm principles undergo in this play.

The most economical way to track through the mesh of words of which *King Lear* is made is to follow the recurrent image clusters through scene by scene. Each cluster has its own fruit, but each cluster is linked to the other clusters. We have to think of them separately at first in order to recognize all the particular fruit, the words which embody the images. Then we have to trace the linkages between each cluster. Finally, and most important, we have to study the growth and change of the images as the play's story develops.

The most prominent cluster of images relates to nature in its two chief manifestations, human or bestial nature and the natural order. The storm in the world of nature dominates the middle of the play. It is an atmospheric symbol of the disorder Lear has introduced into the kingdom by his act of dividing his rule between his sons-in-law. True nature is the 'bond' which

Cordelia declares she observes in her love for her father, and which Lear cannot recognize. Without such bonds, the other nature takes over. Edmund praises the nature which looks after its own interests. It manifests itself in materialistic competition of brother against brother, and in the lechery which sets sister against sister. Lear attaches many animal images to Goneril and Regan. Despite the fact that Goneril is the first to mention lechery, in Lear's riotous followers, Lear characterizes her fault as a consequence of the animal passions. Woman is a centaur. 'To the girdle do the gods inherit, / Beneath is all the fiend's.' The Fool says 'Truth's a dog must to kennel; he must be whipped out when the Lady Brach [bitch] may stand by the fire and stink.' Humans show their animal nature in their smell, and references to smelling augment the image cluster of nature. When Gloucester wants to kiss Lear's hand in token of his renewed allegiance, Lear says 'Let me wipe it first; it smells of mortality.' Gloucester's reaction to that reminder is 'O ruined piece of nature!'

Closely related to the nature cluster are two others: necessity and madness. Necessity becomes Lear's preoccupation when he is deprived of all his material assets and is joined by naked Tom on the stormy heath. To Regan he had protested 'O reason not the need', and 'Allow not nature more than nature needs'. On the heath, seeing Edgar disguised as Tom a Bedlam in no more than a blanket, he says 'Unaccommodated man is no more but such a poor, bare, forked animal as thou art' and starts to take off his own clothes. Clothing becomes an image of human selfishness and deceit: 'robes and furred gowns hide all'. Necessity comes down to naked man. The irony that the naked man on the heath is himself in disguise as a madman links the images of necessity to madness. When Lear urges Regan not to 'reason' the need for stripping his followers down to nothing he invokes two levels of reason. At one level is the commonsensical and materialistic arguments the two sisters use to justify their actions in stripping Lear. At the other is the insight into the truth that must to kennel while the lady bitches can stand in the warmth of the fireside. Only when Lear is mad does he see the truth about human necessity which Cordelia, Kent and the Fool have been trying to tell him for so long.

Madness is shown in a variety of forms. It begins in the Fool's handy-dandy, his satirical inversions of the truth. It is extended through Poor Tom's pretended lunacies. Centrally it is Lear's own progress from the blindness of his initial position of reason through the loss of everything, including his reason, to the madness by which he sees the truth. This reversal is parallelled graphically in Gloucester, who only begins to see when he is blinded. The clustered image-patterns of light and darkness, reason and madness, sight and insight all follow the same path through the play. Images of nakedness set against clothing and disguise, of animal nature set against spiritual good, indeed all the images in the play fit into these interlinked clusters. When Lear in his madness says 'a dog's obeyed in office' he joins the image of animality with the disguise of the furred robes of justice. Similarly saying that Cordelia's tears are pearls or Gloucester's lost eyes 'precious stones' inverts traditional materialistic valuation. Such inversions emphasize the variety of paradoxes in the play, the contrary definitions of worth, the two natures of animal and moral humankind, the distinction of sight from insight and reason from sanity. And at the same time they are all elaborations of the disorder in nature.

Any passage from the play will show aspects of these image clusters, and will ripple with the tensions generated by their links with the other uses elsewhere in the play. No other play of Shakespeare's is so tightly written in the economy and inter-connectedness of its images and the pervasiveness of their application. Any passage could illustrate this. One in particular, where the blinded Gloucester meets the mad Lear (IV.vi) has already been cited three times in this brief account of the image clusters.

[*Lear*] Here's money for thee.
He gives flowers.
Gloucester. O, let me kiss that hand!
Lear. Let me wipe it first; it smells of mortality.
Gloucester. O ruined piece of nature! This great world
   Shall so wear out to naught. Dost thou know me?
Lear. I remember thine eyes well enough. Dost thou squiny at me? No,
   do thy worst, blind Cupid; I'll not love. Read thou this challenge;
   mark but the penning of it.
Gloucester. Were all thy letters suns, I could not see.
Edgar. I would not take this from report. It is;
   And my heart breaks at it.
Lear. Read.
Gloucester. What, with the case of eyes?

Lear. O, ho, are you there with me? No eyes in your head, nor no money in your purse? Your eyes are in a heavy case, your purse in a light; yet you see how this world goes.

Gloucester. I see it feelingly.

Lear. What, art mad? A man may see how this world goes, with no eyes. Look with thine ears. See how yon justice rails upon yon simple thief. Hark in thine ear – change places, and, handy-dandy, which is the justice, which is the thief? Thou hast seen a farmer's dog bark at a beggar?

Gloucester. Ay, sir.

Lear. And the creature run from the cur? There thou mightst behold the great image of authority: a dog's obeyed in office.
Thou rascal beadle, hold thy bloody hand.
Why dost thou lash that whore? Strip thy own back.
Thou hotly lusts to use her in that kind
For which thou whipp'st her. The usurer hangs the cozener.
Through tattered clothes great vices do appear.
Robes and furred gowns hide all. Plate sins with gold,
And the strong lance of justice hurtless breaks;
Arm it in rags, a pygmy's straw does pierce it.

Every phrase in this passage belongs to one or other of the great image clusters in this play. Each additional use enlarges the cluster and extends its links with the other clusters. No image is offered with the randomness of true madness.

The first action is visual rather than verbal. Lear is like Edgar, stripped of all his material rights. Edgar has covered his nakedness with a blanket, Lear with wild flowers. The stage direction for his entry in this scene reads in the Folio text '*Enter Lear fantastically dressed with wild flowers*' (the Quarto version reads '*Enter Lear mad*'). Instead of money he gives Gloucester what he has, an emblem of the natural world, some of his flowers. He calls them money because he is confused between the values of the old world in which he owned everything of material value, and the new world of his nakedness. Gloucester's immediate reaction is to renew his old loyalty, his bond of nature, by the standard act of kissing his master's hand. Lear pauses over this because he knows now that he is human before he is royal. He also senses, despite his own answer to Gloucester's first question where he says he is 'every inch a king', that his authority now sits on him oddly. This scene sets a maltreated subject in front of the king whose misjudgements have caused the maltreatment. Lear is struggling to understand the nature his actions have released.

Gloucester, now blinded, has more insight than Lear at this point. He sees Lear as a piece, and a masterpiece, of nature brought to ruin. In this he is a microcosm of the whole world's ruin – 'this great world / Shall so wear out to naught.' Lear, however, refuses to recognize Gloucester. He identifies the blind eyes incongruously as belonging to Cupid, emblem of lechery. He tests Gloucester's blindness by urging him to read a challenge, a visual anticipation of Edgar's written challenge to his unnatural brother. In Lear's case the challenge is his own fantastical attempt to confront the forces he has unleashed, symbolized by both Gloucester and blind Cupid. Gloucester tries a weak joke in reply to Lear's demand, the 'case' of eyes meaning both the hollow sockets and the sorry case his blindness now shows. Lear promptly seizes on the joke as a mark of their similar plights. Gloucester is 'with me'. Both are blinded and therefore now 'see how this world goes'. Gloucester again jokes desperately, anticipating his own later prayer to the gods to 'Let the superfluous and lust-dieted man . . . that will not see / Because he does not feel, feel your power quickly!' Lear is unconvinced. He cannot believe that others have long since seen what he now recognizes. He launches at Gloucester again with examples of the handy-dandy world of nature.

His examples all stress the similarity of the animal aspects of human nature under the assortment of clothing that humanity wears. Clothes are a disguise for the sameness of humanity. The justice and the thief are indistinguishable. The beadle punishes the whore for the lusts he feels himself. The only difference is that the clothes of high social status conceal and therefore protect the smelly humanity beneath. This is Lear's interpretation of the evidence he has been given by his 'dog-hearted daughters'. He is overwhelmed by a feeling of injustice, and lectures his unjustly punished hearer on the subject with all the force of a new convert to the view.

Edgar, still naked but for his blanket, is the sole witness to this confrontation. Visually his disguise of madness covers a perfect understanding. His aside is the good man's reaction to the ruin of the two men's natures that he sees. The king is mad, the subject has been blinded by that madness. 'It is; / And my heart breaks at it.' This is things as they are. They exemplify the storm in nature. Lear's words in his madness are like the

Fool's legerdemain, his 'handy-dandy' or sleight of hand with the truth. Edgar later affirms that he speaks 'reason in madness', 'matter and impertinency mixed'. Lear's version of 'how this world goes' is cynical, of course. This world of animal natures is not the other world of natural order, the utopia which stands in steady contrast to the dystopia which Lear unleashes in the play.

Lear, of course, is wrong. His violent anger, which first showed itself against Cordelia and Kent, then against the other two daughters, and now against all humanity, is born out of his own feeling of self-righteousness. He does not yet see himself as responsible for the nakedness he and his two companions now suffer. This passage marks only one step in Lear's progress. He now sees the point of the Fool's handy-dandy, the paradoxes by which this world goes. In his previous appearance on stage he had attempted to hold a trial of his disloyal daughters, represented by joint-stools. Now he dismisses all justice, on the grounds that a judge is not different from a thief, and he ends the scene with a cry for universal punishment, howling 'Kill, kill, kill, kill, kill!' When the gentleman appears from Cordelia he assumes that he is to be imprisoned, despite the way they emphasize that he is still a king. He runs off to escape the responsibility that name re-imposes on him, concerned above all as it is with the administration of justice. He has still a long way to go.

The images which shape this play grow and change with each recurrence. The word 'nothing', for instance, which belongs to the imagery of material and spiritual wealth, is such an ordinary word that its repeated use in its special contexts alienates us from its ordinary meaning. Each use adds to the earlier meanings, so that it becomes a set of milestones showing how far the situation has changed each time it recurs. 'Nature', the most basic of the key words in the play, occurs much more frequently – it is used altogether forty times. That very frequency makes it both a static motif word, a recurrent reminder of the central concept at issue, and a mark of the changes.

The first time 'nothing' is heard in the play is Cordelia's abrupt and taciturn reply to Lear's elaborate and ceremonial invitation to her to give voice to her love so that she can be given a more opulent reward than her sisters. After a scene in which material wealth is so flaunted along with Lear's mathematical calculations of it all, the divisions he has drawn on the map, the word comes as a shock. It echoes four more times before Lear invites her to say something more profitable. Cordelia has already murmured in an aside that she can only love and be silent, and her 'nothing' is the nearest she can come to silence. Lear takes it very materialistically, as the original no-thing. There is no immaculate conception. She must speak if she is to win the things he has planned to award her. Forced to reply, she takes refuge in a deliberate twisting of words to point out that he is trying to measure the immeasurable. She employs his own mistaken language, calling her love a 'bond', to indicate that Lear misinterprets even the bond of natural love as if it were a legal contract. More openly sarcastic, she parodies his materialistic calculations of quantities of love by arguing that her sisters must have a poor relationship with their husbands if their father has all their love. But Lear is uncomprehending.

Gloucester is equally uncomprehending in the next scene, when Edmund uses the same word to tantalize him into demanding to see the letter which has forged in Edgar's handwriting. This paper is indeed a 'nothing' which Gloucester misreads as easily as Lear misread Cordelia's word. It is a lie, a nothing of which he makes a great deal. When Gloucester says 'If it be nothing I shall not need spectacles' he speaks more prophetically than he knows. Both plots are launched by these two misinterpretations of the one blank word.

These first uses of the word do not invite a close inspection. It is such an ordinary word that its repetition, while emphatic, does not at first lead us to question exactly what it means in these early contexts. Later uses reflect back on the first occurrences, and relate it more closely to the difference between material and spiritual wealth which France first stressed. In I.iv Lear actually repeats the tag from Lucretius to the Fool when Kent calls the Fool's speech of wisdom nothing and the Fool asks Lear what use he can make of it. The Fool is developing Cordelia's game of sarcasm into parodic inversions of the truth, with the same object of teaching Lear wisdom. His own concern is more materialistic, however. He directs attention to the fact that Lear has forsaken his power and responsibility with his wealth. Lear himself is now nothing. He has split his wisdom in the middle and given both halves to his daughters, leaving nothing for himself. The Fool is therefore the better man, being a Fool while Lear is nothing.

Goneril, who has entered to hear this last crack at Lear's foolishness, has remained silent, in an ironic renewal of Cordelia's initial tactic. The Fool reminds us of that when he acknowledges that Goneril disapproves of his babble, and he must stop speaking – 'your face bids me, though you say nothing.' Silence is not nothing, whatever Edmund's forged letter may be. Silence speaks, while words can be nothing. A little later, in II.i, Edmund in fact uses the same phrase to Edgar that the Fool had used of Goneril when he teases his incomprehension by asking 'Have you nothing said . . . 'gainst the Duke of Albany?'

In the second act the word divides into its alternative significances. Kent and Edgar stay with the first meaning. When Kent announces his hope in Cordelia at the end of II.ii he says 'Nothing almost sees miracles / But misery', a curious phrasing which by its inversion emphasizes the word which Cordelia was the first to use, while relating her to a miraculous redemption from the present misery. Edgar's misery is more bluntly but also more ambiguously put. If he disguises himself as Poor Tom 'That's something yet: Edgar I nothing am' (II.iii). He is Edgar, and nothing. He is not Edgar.

Both Kent and Edgar here relate the 'no-thing' which signifies spiritual worth back to Cordelia's first use of the term. Kent, however, in the same scene picks up the other meaning, giving it another form to distinguish it from its spiritual significance. Kent first broaches it in his invective addressed to Cornwall against Oswald in II.ii, when he speaks of him as 'Knowing naught – like dogs – but following.' This animal ignorance is the materialism which characterizes Goneril and Regan. The word 'naught', which was also used with the special connotation of lechery, is now applied to both daughters. Lear uses it of Goneril in II.iv, and Gloucester calls Regan a 'naughty lady' when she plucks his beard in III.vii. Theirs is the negation which is the paradoxical opposite to Cordelia's no-thing.

In Act III these distinctions are maintained and re-emphasized. Gloucester uses Edmund's 'nothing', the eloquent silence, when he urges him not to speak about the letter he has received (III.iii). Lear is given an ironical use when, after outshouting the storm, he says 'I will be the pattern of all patience. / I will say nothing.' This is Gloucester's nothing, but by the association Lear gives it to Christian patience it is also

Cordelia's spiritual quality. The irony lies in the impossibility at this point of Lear keeping to his own claim. He has still some angry way to go before the admission, in IV.vi, that he is indeed a fool, and responsible for his own misfortunes. In III.iv, seeing Edgar as Tom, he claims that nothing could have brought such a figure to his nakedness and madness but his daughters. His statement about unaccommodated man, the naked figure who defines necessity, is preceded by his recognition, in the person of Mad Tom, of the opposite to his nothing: 'Thou art the thing itself!' Humanity, even in such a mad and naked wretch as Poor Tom, is not no-thing.

In Act IV, the word disappears. Once Lear has awoken from his sleep and has recovered his sanity enough to know his own foolishness it is never used again in the rest of the play. Just as Edgar recovers his clothing in Act IV, and with it his control over events, so Lear recovers his clothing once he has recognized the true significance of no-thing. The point of nakedness and being dressed in wild flowers belongs with the storm and the process of being stripped of everything. After that, apart from the final twist of Lear's last deprivation, the loss of Cordelia's life, the path is upward. The point of the spiritual nothing and the naughty lechery has served its turn. In the conclusion the true echo of 'nothing' is Lear's 'Never, never, never, never, never,' his recognition that there will be no second coming for Cordelia.

This attempt at analysing the imagery in one play says hardly anything about the use of language in its own right. It treats the poetry of the plays mainly as components in the dramatic story, instruments to further the plot. It takes no account either of the superb eloquence of Isabella's speeches pleading with Angelo or the magnificent comic backchat in Falstaff's early prose scenes with Prince Hal. In all of Shakespeare's plays the central point of access is the language, whether it is read on the page or heard in the mouths of modern actors. We tend therefore to take note of its precision and treat its beauty as an incidental bonus. At the same time, no one line or speech can really be taken in isolation from the play which provides its context. Holism is a necessary aim even when it is the words alone that require attention. A close study of the language of even one play would require a space far greater than this book occupies.

6 Dramatic Forms

Procrustes, a figure in Greek legend, was a robber with a bed which was supposed to be magic, since it was always exactly the right size for all his guests. The point of the story was that he made them the right size either by cutting off their feet or stretching them on a rack. The Procrustean bed is an apt image for the genres of tragedy, comedy, history or tragicomedy, because the definition of each genre distorts the plays to fit it. Genres have their uses, but it is necessary to be careful to adjust the genre, rather than the plays in it.

Byron in *Don Juan* once satirically summed up the basic genres: 'All tragedies are finished by a death, / All comedies are ended by a marriage'. Shakespeare had a distinct definition of his own for tragedy. Like Byron's, it was pretty minimal. His uses of the word in his plays always seem to indicate the same thing: a story which ends in the death of the central character. All of his tragedies, and those of the history plays which were labelled 'tragical histories' end in that way. He seems, however, to have had less consistency in his idea of comedy. Most of the comedies in his canon do end in marriage, which many readers take to be the basic definition for the 'romantic comedy' genre. And yet *The Taming of the Shrew* does not end but starts with a marriage, while *Love's Labours Lost* closes with the male lovers punished, and the postponement of any more wooing for a year and a day. Of the so-called problem comedies *All's Well that Ends Well* closes with a marriage, but it is an alliance that has a large question mark against it. Similarly *Measure for Measure* ends with a proposal of marriage which its recipient answers with silence. On the whole Shakespeare avoided the alternative concept of comedy current in his time, Jonsonian satire (though *Love's Labours Lost* comes very close to it), and kept to comedies in which love is the central impetus. But no two of the comedies are alike. There is as much variety in the comedies as there is in the tragedies. What is more these doubts about a generic definition of the comedies take no account of the romances, the last plays, just as the standard definition of Shakespearean tragedy sets aside the plays set in English history, and even leaves in doubt the Roman plays, *Julius Caesar, Coriolanus* and *Antony and Cleopatra*.

The business of identifying the Shakespearean genres is really more to do with critical games than with Shakespeare's plays. By defining the genre of a particular play one can set up a holistic view of it while at the same time fitting it into a familiar pattern. With a normative view of what tragedy is one has a ready-made shape which makes the story of, say, King Lear more easily recognizable. Any variation from the normative shape will help to clarify the distinctive features of a particular play. It is implicitly a comparative exercise, contrasting the normative shape with the perceived shape of the individual play in order to strengthen one's understanding of the uniqueness of the play being studied. There is some value in this. The danger in it appears when the concept of the genre is too strong, and becomes a Procrustean bed for the individual play.

Critics have been writing about tragedy since Aristotle, to the point where it has become a philosophical principle, as well as a yardstick for great drama. In Aristotle's Greece tragedies were performed at religious festivals, as retellings of familiar myths. The philosophy of ancient Greece was fatalistic, at least in so far as it assumed that human life was subject to powers, natural and supernatural, which were beyond human control. Natural disasters such as earthquakes, or human errors when a man kills his father and marries his mother in ignorance of who they are, had to be not only endured but somehow explained, or if not explained then somehow accommodated. Fatalism was the clearest answer. The gods play their games, and humanity becomes their victims. Tragedy became a means not just of explaining the inexplicable accidents of life, but of generating a sense of fatalistic resignation about such accidents.

Human society has changed a great deal since the philosophy of ancient Greece gave rise to tragedy as a religious and dramatic form. Divine intervention in human activities is regarded much more sceptically. Even in *King Lear* while different characters may constantly invoke the gods there is never any sign of the gods themselves intervening. Everything happens exclusively on the earthly level. Shakespeare's tragedy has moved on from the Greek form, though at its core it still poses a similar question. But since Shakespeare European culture has changed sharply. The writing of tragedies as a dramatic form has largely disappeared, and we have experienced the paradoxical 'death of tragedy'. Along with that death, though, and perhaps partly as a result, there has been a renewed curiosity about tragic philosophy, and a re-reading amounting almost to rewriting both of Greek tragedy and Shakespearean tragedy to get them to meet the changed modern needs. It is this rewriting which causes most of the difficulties in the generic approach to Shakespeare. Shakespearean tragedy, especially as manifest in *King Lear*, has become almost a modern philosophical paradigm.

The philosophy of tragedy usually involves coming to terms with death. This may entail the question of personal justification for the death – the hero's responsibility for his actions – or it may entail confrontation with its apparent arbitrariness or unfairness. As a form, tragedy is usually elevated in critical opinion higher than melodrama, which treats death as accidental or malevolent, and higher than morality plays, which treat death as a direct enactment of God's justice. Tragedy must contain, philosophically, more than the simple pattern of crime and punishment or sin and repentance which belongs with those related but less complex forms. A better understanding of the meaning of death, which tragedy is supposed to give, implies a better understanding of the meaning of life.

It is well to deal with the larger philosophical questions about tragedy fairly sceptically. Approaching *King Lear* with a presupposition about tragedy invites the reading of all too simple lessons from the play. Normally, for instance, preoccupation with the concept of tragedy invites a close focus on the tragic hero, the figure who initiates the tragedy and whose death is an acceptance of responsibility for the crisis. We may follow through the story of King Lear as the play's hero, from his initial responsibility for dividing his kingdom, the decision which leads to all the disasters that follow, to his death, the ultimate punishment for his mistake. That simple pattern leaves out of account first the death of Cordelia, an utterly innocent victim of his mistake, and secondly it leaves Albany's last acts out of account. Albany, the last survivor of Lear's heirs, ends the play trying to do exactly what led to the tragedy in the outset. He tries to abdicate as Lear had done, and divide the kingdom again, between Kent and Edgar. It is only the accident of Kent's refusal that saves him from repeating Lear's mistake. Too close a focus on the death of Lear as the tragic hero will prevent these other features of the play's conclusion from being taken into account.

Elizabethan audiences had a simple guide to channel their expectation about a new play. If the players wanted to give their customers an advance signal of what to expect, they could hang black curtains across the tiring-house wall at the back of the stage. In a play performed at Shakespeare's Globe in 1599 one of the first characters to enter says 'the stage is hung with black, and I perceive / The auditors prepared for tragedy.' A contemporary drawing of an indoor playhouse shows hangings decorated with a figure of Cupid with his bow, presumably a suitable backcloth for a romantic comedy. Such signals about the genre were unambiguous, more so on the whole than the plays which they represented.

King Lear is a tragedy, but it is better to see the play defining its own concept of tragedy than tragedy as defining the play. The question of its nature as a Christian play is central to this. It has been argued, for instance, that one of the reasons for the death of tragedy was that it was antithetical to Christianity. Tragedy, rooted in classical Greece, makes no allowance for the prospect of heaven and hell in the afterlife. The prospect of reward in heaven or punishment in hell makes nonsense of the idea of death as itself a consequence of transgression in life. Originally tragedy was little concerned with moral transgression. Aristotle used the term 'hamartia' for the mistake or error which usually leads the hero to his doom. Nineteenth-century translators of Aristotle called it a flaw, or moral weakness, superadding a Christian gloss of moral responsibility which the Greeks never acknowledged. *King Lear* stands at some distance from Greek tragedy in this respect. But its Christianity is also peculiar.

It is a play which clearly divides the good children from the evil. The evil children all die, and with them the evil son-in-law. But the good Cordelia also dies. Above all Lear himself, an all-too-innocent party to the wrongs he does which initiate the tragedy, is punished to the point where his world becomes a torture chamber. On his death Kent says 'He hates him / That would upon the rack of this tough world / Stretch him out longer.' There is no heavenly justice apparent in this play.

Despite the fact that the play is specifically set in pre-Christian Britain, *King Lear* is full of biblical echoes. Not only is Cordelia said to be a redeemer, but she echoes Christ's words when she says in IV.iv 'O dear father, / It is thy business that I go about.' She is indeed doing Lear's work for him, in bringing the good French army to confront the evil forces of her sisters. Good, though, does not triumph in the battle. Ultimately, in her material poverty of imprisonment and her spiritual riches, Cordelia comes to represent Christ at the crucifixion. Crucifixion was a Roman punishment for criminals, a form of hanging, while at the same time it was the act of Christ which made the redemption of humankind possible. These features of the play relating Cordelia to Christ have to be set against, and indeed distinguished from, the constant invocation of the pagan gods by different characters in this play.

All the calls made by different characters on the gods get no response. They say more about the state of mind of the characters making them than about destiny or divine intervention. Gloucester's despair is marked by his claim that the gods kill men for their sport. The happy ending to Edgar's story is marked by his declaration, after overcoming Edmund in the duel, that 'The gods are just, and of our pleasant vices / Make instruments to plague us.' Albany, the most obtuse figure in the play, calls the deaths of Goneril and Regan a 'judgement of the heavens' only a few lines before Cordelia's body is brought on stage to join those of her sisters. There is no cause to believe any of the earthly characters in the play when they speak about the gods. And in the story of the play, the crucial question about divine judgement is raised by the one major change Shakespeare introduced to his sources, so that instead of Lear surviving to live with Cordelia, she dies, as Christ did. If this is tragic philosophy, it works in the same way that the Christian interpretation of the central mystery of the crucifixion works. The death of Cordelia is a fact which is at the same time an earthly enigma, akin to the mystery of the crucifixion. It does not easily match any of the familiar patterns either of Greek fatalism or modern materialism. It does not even urge a

Christian gloss on the events of the play. Like the crucifixion it is there, to be accommodated as it best can be, according to human interpretation and familiar experience.

Horace Walpole once said that life is a comedy to those who think, and a tragedy to those who feel. This is true in more than one sense, since we laugh at comic characters but feel with tragic heroes, and we rationalize comedy, feeling safely distanced from the figures we laugh at, more readily than we can tragedy. The audience at a comedy has to feel itself to be slightly superior to, and therefore distant from, the comic figures, even the romantic leads, if it is to be able to laugh at their follies. By contrast the audience at a tragedy has to feel sympathy for and kinship with the central characters, however catastrophically mistaken their actions.

This distinction between the two genres has some important effects. Comedy is a corporate activity. The audience has to feel itself to be a community which laughs together. Tragedy is more personal and therefore isolating. The cynic who wrote 'laugh, and the world laughs with you; cry, and you weep alone' was undoubtedly a theatregoer. In Shakespeare's plays this distinction has the effect of isolating the characters at the end of his tragedies, and uniting them at the end of the comedies. Shakespearean tragedy emphasizes individuality. His comedy emphasizes human beings as social animals. However much Byron may have been misogynistic when he stressed the verb by writing that all comedy is ended by a marriage, that ceremony certainly operates in Shakespearean comedy as a mark of re-established social harmony. The collective laughter which signals a community among the audience is reflected in the community re-united by the closure of the comedies. A laughing audience will rate the life of solitary meditation which made the Duke neglect his judicial duties in *Measure for Measure* and the urge to withdraw from society which took Isabella to the Poor Clares' doorstep, as distinctly inferior to life within society.

It is not just a practical point about the writer's biography and working habits to note that Shakespeare seems to have written more or less one comedy and one tragedy or history play each year of his working life in London. Possibly that was what he was contracted to supply to his company of players. The idea is important because it makes the only really valid point about the various genres and sub-genres within the

Shakespeare canon that stands up to close scrutiny. Critics have found various subdivisions of comedy in Shakespeare: early comedies, middle comedies, problem or 'dark' comedies and late romances or tragicomedies. All these stand together under the same umbrella term. Attempts to make some comedies out to be darker than others, and even to make some of them tragicomedies, fall prey to the worst pitfalls of genre criticism. *Measure for Measure* in particular is prone to this kind of problem. Written in about 1603, it seems to have been the last of the comedies Shakespeare wrote before *Pericles,* the first of the romances or tragicomedies, which was on stage in 1607. That four-year gap, when Shakespeare wrote no comedies, only *King Lear, Macbeth* and *Timon of Athens,* has helped to make critics susceptible to the idea of a darkened Shakespeare who had finally lost the ability to write comic plays. Such a view makes it easy to interpret *Measure for Measure* as a dark play, much more a tragicomedy than a truly funny play like the comedies which were written in the years before, *As You Like It, Twelfth Night,* and *The Merry Wives of Windsor.*

In my view *Measure for Measure* is as straightforwardly a comedy as any of the Shakespeare plays. The Duke and Isabella are as vulnerable to the audience's indulgent laughter as Lucio or Pompey. Isabella, with her sigh of adoration for 'the sisterhood, the votarists of Saint Clare', is a comic figure, even in these first lines. The Duke is similarly a comic figure as his privacy is invaded by the reality of Vienna's street life when he talks in disguise with Lucio and hears of the rake's intimacy with the city's vanished ruler. The play certainly does have the threat of death lodged heavily in its plot. Claudio, Barnardine, Angelo and Lucio are all threatened with execution at one point or another. But a promise of execution that Barnardine can refuse because he is suffering from a hang-over after a night's heavy drinking in the prison is hardly a serious threat. The play can easily be darkened by being performed darkly, like all of Shakespeare's comedies. If the Duke is played seriously, especially as the quasi-divine controlling force that he was commonly taken to be in the nineteenth century, much of the comedy disappears along with most of the point of the story as a learning exercise for the Duke and Isabella. To take it that way is to squeeze the play into a sub-genre which it cannot be made to fit, and in the process to lose its intrinsically comic structure.

The plays based on English history were Shakespeare's most consistent and concerted attempts at fulfilling his commitment for 'serious' plays before he began to write the great tragedies. Before *Hamlet* the only tragedies he wrote were *Titus Andronicus, Romeo and Juliet,* and *Julius Caesar,* and even *Julius Caesar* seems to have been conceived initially as the first of a new series of plays about Roman history, following the completion of the English history series with *Henry V.* These history plays do not follow the tragic structure of the 'central' tragedies like *Hamlet* and *King Lear.* Indeed to some extent Shakespeare seems to have actively avoided a tragic structure for any of the history plays. *Richard II*, which could have been written as Richard's tragedy, is based on a precise balance of the falling Richard against the rising Henry. *Julius Caesar*, which might have been the tragedy of Julius, kills him in the middle of the play and then concentrates on the two survivors, Brutus and Antony. In neither play can the figure who dies at the conclusion, Richard and Brutus, be called a tragic hero without narrowing the focus so far as to exclude almost all the play's main concerns.

The main concerns of the English and Roman history plays lie somewhere between the individual focus of the tragedies and the social space of the comedies. Shakespearean drama with its multitude of characters of course invites consideration of the individual in society much more readily than the individual alone. The focus on rulers and the problems of rule in the history plays asks for attention to be directed to the interaction between individual personalities and the social environment within which those individuals move. To a great extent it actively avoids consideration of a single individual personality. Prince Hal is the necessary focus of attention as the heir apparent in a monarchy where the personality of the ruler is crucial to the wellbeing of the state. If we take the point of the gloss in *Measure for Measure* on the biblical tag about judges, the character of the state's supreme judge and lawgiver must be seen as a basic political question. But the personality of the potential ruler is the focus for a broader consideration of rule and its consequences both in the society of the court and in the Eastcheap tavern.

The middle position of the history plays, between the focus of the tragedies on individuals and the social focus of the comedies, makes the structure of *1 Henry IV* especially apt.

The serious question is Hal's honour. Hotspur stands in the main plot as a gauge for Hal's own definition of it. The comic question is there in the subplot, with Falstaff. It is not an easily divisible structure, though. Hotspur's fantastical extravagances are themselves comic, beyond the scale of the prince's burlesques of them. And under the comedy of Falstaff's pleas not to be banished his Harry's company there is a profound pathos, not just for the fat knight but for the dehumanizing of the prince which such a cool withdrawal will entail. The history plays are supremely of this world, and human frailty is the stuffing of both comedy and tragedy.

All three of the plays used as case studies here are of this world. Cordelia is called a redeemer, but that is a human gloss on her conduct. The Duke of Vienna may announce that 'He who the sword of heaven will bear / Should be as holy as severe', but his attempts at swinging the sword of justice are distinctly human. Hotspur and Falstaff may flank the prince like tempters in a medieval morality play, but he exploits them both in an emphatically human and self-interested way. There are serious, even potentially tragic elements in all the plays, and comic elements too, depending on the focus the story gives them. The history play makes no overt claim to the philosophical pretensions of tragedy, but in its study of the conflict between individual and social will, pleasure and duty, altruism and self-interest in the heir to the throne it has as much weight of philosophy as it has comedy. To a great extent tragedy and comedy are preconditions, a matter of audience expectation based on nothing more weighty than the colour of the stage hangings. What follows is a choice of focus.

7 Word and Character

One of the main qualities of the drama as a literary form is that it conceals the voice of its author more completely than is usual in either poetry or the novel. This has, for our purposes, two main consequences. First, it requires the author to construct his characters in words, and to make the words fit the characters. Secondly, it leaves the author's own position and what he is trying to communicate through his work thoroughly problematic. It is dangerous to assume that the author speaks through the mouth of any one character. Therefore only in the total construct of the play can the author's vision be recognized. We come back to the holistic approach.

No single statement anywhere in any of these plays can be taken as anything but the thoughts of the character at the moment of speaking. That notorious declaration of Gloucester's, that 'As flies to wanton boys are we to the gods: / They kill us for their sport' used to be taken as the essential 'message' of *King Lear*. Apart from the point that it is futile to look for simple 'messages' in any literary text, this view ignores the fact that the statement exactly fits Gloucester's frame of mind at the moment he says it. His mentality is not only gullible, but passive. His early speech to Edmund, that 'these late eclipses in the sun and moon portend no good to us' is a fatalistic expression of submission to an arbitrary destiny. The sufferings that he then undergoes lead him to conclude that the gods are indeed arbitrary, and hence to the despair which makes him attempt to commit suicide. After this statement Edgar's rescue helps him to change his mind. When he dies he is no longer despairing and no longer believes in arbitrary fate. Every statement in a Shakespeare play is contingent on the circumstances of the utterer and the moment of utterance.

This is an important point, because one of the most seductive

ways of trying to comprehend a play in its entirety is to identify with a single central character, and take that character's
statements as the truth. In this, the tragedies can be misleading. The comedies offer a better guide. Lear is the inescapable
focus of his tragedy. We follow his path through the storm in
nature, and end with his unbearable confrontation of the fact
of Cordelia's death. We share his experience. Prince Hal in
the history play similarly commands attention first, though
increasingly we are drawn towards Falstaff. But in *Measure for
Measure*, while the Duke and Isabella share the main focus,
they do not command the same intimate sympathy that a
tragic hero does. What is more, their stories run separately for
most of the way, only converging properly at the finale. We see
them from further off. This distancing, which is inherent in
comedy, makes identification with any character a less intimate and less directly emotional matter than in tragedy. When
Isabella argues with herself over Angelo's demand, and con-
cludes 'More than our brother is our chastity', she is at a greater
remove from the audience's sympathy than Lear at any step in
the sequence of his mistakes. The point to note is that much of
what applies to the comic characters should also be applied in
the tragedy. Too close an identification with any one character
can be misleading.

Perhaps the best way to put Lear as the focal figure into a
broader perspective would be to examine a lesser figure in the
play, Lear's successor. The Duke of Albany seems to have
posed problems for Shakespeare, because he altered the shape
of the role when he revised the play a few years after its first
performance. In the revision Shakespeare gave Albany less to
say about the gradual shifts in his attitude, but strengthened
his function as a critical observer and commentator on the
events of the play. Although he is at first indistinguishable from
Cornwall as one of Lear's two sons-in-law, by the end of the
play he is clearly an opposite to Cornwall. The two figures are
strongly differentiated. Cornwall is short-tempered and curt in
his speech, while Albany is slow and hesitant. His wife Goneril
scorns him and is openly dismissive every time he tries to
speak in the early acts, calling him 'a milk-livered man', and
urging him to get on with his duty of defending the realm
against the French invaders. She brushes aside impatiently his
half-hearted protests against her treatment of her father.
Twice we hear of rumours that Albany and Cornwall are at

odds, but nothing seems to come of it, since Albany joins Goneril, Regan and Edmund in fighting against Cordelia's forces. He does not emerge as a significant figure, and a participant on the side of the 'good' against the evil characters, until the final act.

In the final act he takes over control, as suits the duke who has won victory in the battle. His very name suits a ruler of ancient England, which the Fool gives the old mythical title 'the realm of Albion'. Albany supports Edgar in reasserting the rule of virtue over his wife and Edmund. Throughout the final scene he tries to assert the forms of normality, as we might expect from a good man. He has also been moved some distance along the road Lear has travelled. When he hears of the deaths of his wife and Regan he echoes Aristotle, who spoke of tragedy moving fear and pity in the audience, saying 'This judgement of the heavens that makes us tremble / Touches us not with pity.' In his interpretation, the fear that Aristotle identified in the conclusion of a tragedy comes from the death of the bad, while the pity is for the good. Thus the entry of Lear with dead Cordelia a few moments later supplies the pity. Faced with that, Albany tries to restore the old order by giving Lear back his crown and promising to reward the good and punish the bad. But both of these orderly thoughts prove pointless, as has been noted above, when set against the fact of Cordelia's murder. The inadequacy of the ordinary man faced with such a monstrosity is confirmed by Albany's final attempt to assert authority by repeating Lear's error and dividing the kingdom between Kent and Edgar. The realm is still at risk from ordinariness.

Albany's understanding is less than Lear's, and less than that of any audience which can see his mistakes. His very normality, the slowness of his reaction to Goneril's and Regan's acts, his willingness to do the standard thing, fighting against the invader even when the attacking army is led by Cordelia, and trying to restore the familiar old pattern even with Lear's example in front of him, provides an audience with a yardstick for the abnormality of the tragedy and the necessary abnormality of audience response to it.

In *King Lear* the opening scene, with its formal speeches of flattery and Cordelia's brief reminder that words are not being used for plain truth in them, starts a process which Edmund promptly develops in the second scene, making language part of the pattern of disguise. The Fool's inverted expressions of the truth, given when the plain truth can lead to consequences like Kent's banishment, confirm the value of words as disguise for good as well as evil. But in general the 'good' characters do speak the truth as they see it. In *1 Henry IV* there is no such division of good and bad, truth-tellers and disguisers. There are almost no soliloquies, and the most conspicuous of them, Hal's 'I know you all' speech, is thoroughly open to question. Language in the hands of politicians is a slippery instrument. The history plays lack the clear-cut distinction in their characters between the good and the bad which we find in *King Lear* – in fact *King Lear* is almost the only one of Shakespeare's plays which admits such a clear distinction of moral postures. Therefore the language of any character in the history play is likely to be subject to its speaker's bias and the deceitful circumstances of the story.

The language of Hotspur is a peculiar case here. As a hot-headed, plain-speaking youth concerned with his honour, even if it is the honour of prowess in battle rather than ordinary conduct, he might be expected to speak more directly than most. But he becomes a rebel, and his plainness has to be finely balanced. Shakespeare made him a flamboyant, even truculent youth, whose words express his personality more than they say anything direct, except at a few crucial moments. His first speech, for instance, in I.iii, is supposed to be defensive, an explanation to the king why he has not done what the king demanded. He excuses himself obliquely by claiming that he reacted angrily to the figure who made the demand of him:

> I then, all smarting with my wounds being cold,
> To be so pestered with a popinjay,
> Out of my grief and my impatience
> Answered neglectingly, I know not what,
> He should, or he should not, for he made me mad
> To see him shine so brisk, and smell so sweet,
> And talk so like a waiting-gentlewoman
> Of guns, and drums, and wounds, God save the mark!

Hotspur starts the whole speech with a one-line denial of the king's charge, and then spends thirty-five lines on his reaction to this popinjay before returning to the point with another single-line disclaimer. Blount brings him back to the point, his diplomatic glove concealing an iron hand, when he says that such circumstances must excuse Hotspur's original answer 'so he unsay it now'. Hotspur's evasiveness is put at issue again when he claims that his brother-in-law Mortimer had fought in personal combat with Glendower, and the king denies it.

In the wake of such alternative versions of the truth, it is hardly surprising that when the king has gone Hotspur and his father and uncle should rewrite the history of Richard II's deposition, and set up Mortimer as a rival king to Henry IV. Hotspur's language was celebrated in Shakespeare's time for its belligerence – a comic apprentice in a play of 1607, called on to deliver a 'huffing speech', recites Hotspur's famous lines beginning 'By heaven, methinks it were an easy leap / To pluck bright honour from the pale-faced moon' from this scene (199-204). But that huffing manner should not be allowed to disguise its manipulation of the truth.

A similar liberty through the use of extravagant language to mishandle the truth is evident in *Measure for Measure* in Lucio. In the comedy, however, the trick of disguise allows the Duke to be himself the recipient of Lucio's stories about him. The audience, knowing the truth, enjoys the prospect of Lucio being discomforted when the Duke unmasks himself, and is never given reason to question what the truth is. The Duke's disguise is put on at the same time as the audience is given his reasons for adopting it. Angelo's deception is made clear by the soliloquies in which he announces his problem. In each case the misuse of language for different sorts of disguise is quite clear. In each case it clarifies the personality of the disguiser to the audience, instead of concealing it.

Measure for Measure presents the problem of seeing character through language most strongly, because although at one level the truth is always clear through the various disguises, at another it never is. Both Isabella and the Duke go through learning processes which change their thinking in the course of the play. Their early assertions about their beliefs are therefore falsified as the play goes on, and no direct clue is ever given the audience to prepare them for that. The Duke, even more than Isabella, has been rewritten through a wide range of different interpretations of his personality on stage and amongst the critics. These different views largely vary according to how much he is thought to be in control of events and of himself. He is either a godlike controller of his subjects' lives and fortunes, or a meddling incompetent, depending on how much you believe what he says about himself and his motives. The more dynamic view of the play, as a learning process, of course requires him to begin as a meddling incompetent and end as a godlike controller. By this view his words must slowly acquire more credibility as he comes to learn the truths which the play's story urges on him.

Plays are based on a sequence of dynamic changes, and it is not unreasonable to expect at least the central characters to change along with the changes in the plot. It is therefore likely to be at least in some degreee misleading if we take any single statement from any single point in the progress of the play as the whole truth. Even the conclusion need not offer any conclusive truth, as we can see from the end of *King Lear*, where Albany's attempts to restore normality indicate nothing but his continuing incomprehension. This problem of the limitations inherent in the words of any play inevitably brings us back to the holistic approach. Every speech needs to be kept in its context, not only in the immediate situation in which it is spoken, but in its place in the development of the personality speaking it.

8 Critical Approaches and Further Reading

The variety of different approaches which it is possible to use in getting closer to Shakespeare are all very strongly represented in the mass of published criticism which has appeared in this century. This final chapter will look briefly at some of the publications which have employed the major approaches most notably, and will recommend some of the best examples of each.

Chapter 4 began by looking at the approach which treats the plays as if they were novels. Chapter 5 began with the approach which treats them as poems. Each of these approaches became predominant in turn in the first half of this century. First came the novelistic approach, at its best in the essays of A. C. Bradley, whose *Shakespearean Tragedy* (1904) was ultimately derived from the critical principles of Coleridge, but was also heavily if less obviously influenced by the example of the Victorian novel in its great period through the later nineteenth century. His concern with novelistic realism led him, for instance, to object over the improbability of Edgar writing a letter to his brother when they were living in the same house. Despite that show of literal-mindedness his essays on what he called the four 'central' tragedies, *Hamlet, Othello*, and *Macbeth*, as well as *King Lear*, are still among the finest analyses of Shakespeare's use of the genre, especially as story-telling constructs.

In the 1930s the rise of modernism redirected attention from realism to symbolism, from novels to poetry, and it came to be thought more rewarding to read the plays as if they were poems. The classic statement of this new view was an essay by L. C. Knights, satirically posing the kind of question which used to bother Bradley in its title, 'How Many Children had Lady Macbeth?' (1936). This approach focussed attention on the patterns of imagery, seizing on the discoveries made by Caroline Spurgeon and Wolfgang Clemen, that certain plays used specific clusters of images and used them consistently. It was an approach strongly endorsed by G. Wilson Knight in his 'holistic' analyses. A play that is seen to be organized through a consistent pattern of poetic images rather than as a narrative is easy to read holistically. Some plays of course responded better to the approach through poetic imagery than others, because many of the plays, both early and late, do not have any consistent organizational pattern of images. The status of different plays in critics' minds rose or fell according to how well they fitted the requirements of the poetic approach and the easy access to a holistic view which it provided. The 'central' tragedies, as it happened, are models of this kind of structure. The consensus that these were the greatest of Shakespeare's plays of course therefore gave credibility to this approach, though even within the grouping of the central tragedies reputations shifted. *Hamlet* was the favourite according to the nineteenth-century novelistic approach. *King Lear* replaced it as favourite when the poeticists took over. The poetic approach appeared at its best with a large book on the image patterns in *King Lear* by R. B. Heilman, *This Great Stage* (1952).

This way of reading the plays was entirely consistent with the 'New Criticism' which flourished especially in the USA in the early postwar years. To some extent the 'New Criticism' was a defensive kind of critical stance. It devoted itself to the close reading of the text alone, free from any moral, political or social postures. It regarded significant ambiguity or paradox as the finest kind of poetry, a mode of expression which gave the best possible formulation to the inherent complexity and the problematic nature of any statement. It became a popular way of reading texts because, especially at the height of the Cold War, when patriotism was a political dogma, literature was thought to be accessible only if the reader's position was decidedly neutral. Eventually of course, as political attitudes shifted, it fell into disfavour for precisely the reason that it was ideologically neutral and negative. The aesthetic creed to which the New Criticism attached itself, a version of the old art for art's sake dogma, was discredited in the 1960s.

At first the poeticist approach was challenged by politically and sociologically related theories in a kind of pendulum-swing of opinion which asserted that every form of words is propaganda, and that art for art's sake, the concept of the poem as an end in itself, was a pointless dogma as well as an unattainable one. Eventually much more sophisticated theories of language and discourse came to bear on the idea of reading and criticism, and these inevitably gave rise to new approaches to Shakespeare.

Critics today are agreed on relatively few things about Shakespeare, apart from the unimportance of the question whether it was Shakespeare or Francis Bacon or the Earl of Oxford who wrote the plays. The study of literature is in a state of flux, with few generally agreed principles. As a result (and partly as a cause) it has proved readily responsive to outside influences, whether directly political, as in the 'radical Shakespeare' concept, or indirectly, as in the various 'structuralist' and 'poststructuralist' approaches. It is generally agreed that the riches in the plays are still immensely rewarding, but the variety of ways that have been found to draw on those riches is, to put it mildly, confusing. This variety makes it impossible to use any of the familiar ways of simplifying or schematizing this range. If we presented it as a political spectrum of views from left-wing to right-wing, for instance, we should have to ignore the areas where left and right agree, and (more misleadingly), by the very nature of the concept or metaphor which the terms carry in them, we should find ourselves upholding the illusion that there is a neutral centre somewhere. Consequently the survey of some of the more forceful views that follows will seem, and indeed will largely be, randomly set out, with each individual approach in a separate pigeonhole and therefore not directly related to any other approach.

One of the more radical and influential ideas now current is that who actually wrote the texts is unimportant, and that everything depends on what the reader makes of it, since the reader is the only thing that actually exists. Despite that view, it is well worth beginning this short survey with Samuel Schoenbaum's work on Shakespeare's life. This is worth doing not just because *William Shakespeare. A Compact Documentary Life* (1977) is the most dispassionate and unspeculative biography so far written, but because it was preceded and prepared for by an earlier work, *Shakespeare's Lives* (1970), which surveys three centuries of attempts to identify the original

Shakespeare, and in the process shows how completely each attempt belonged to its own time and the needs of that time. Each age rewrites the biography, as well as the plays.

One distinctive result of the recognition that each age writes its own Shakespeare can be found in *That Shakespeherian Rag: essays on a critical process*, by Terence Hawkes (1986). Hawkes examines the character and the background of a number of major critics and editors of Shakespeare, including Bradley, Dover Wilson, and Walter Raleigh, to show how their own political views came to be reflected in the 'canonical' Shakespeare they created. This position leads logically on to, and largely justifies, the modern shift of focus from the hypothetical (and thoroughly variable) writer to the more tangible and recognizable reader.

For a variety of different reasons the transfer of interest from the writer of the plays to the modern reader has been counterbalanced by an increase in the concern for the immediate context of the plays, the circumstances for which they were originally composed. Marxist critics, critics of the plays as performance texts, and semioticians all concur in this. Their concern is not for the uniqueness of Shakespeare, which is the basis for the biographical interest, but rather his typicality. For Marxists individuality needs to be set in its place in history, while for performance critics and semioticians the intimate familiarity of the author with the players and the audience creates a process of communication which can only be identified through a close understanding of the exact terms which all the original participants shared. This concern appears not only in semiotic studies of language-games in the plays such as Keir Elam's *Shakespeare's Universe of Discourse. Language Games in the Comedies* (1984) and Malcolm Evans's *Signifying Nothing: Truth's True Contents in Shakespeare's Text* (1986), but in many recent studies of the original staging. Of the many such studies which have appeared recently the best is David Bevington's *Action is Eloquence* (1984). More general books about the early theatre, notably Glynne Wickham's four-volume *Early English Stages 1300–1660* (1959–) and Andrew Gurr's much smaller *The Shakespearean Stage 1574–1642* (1980) provide a context in the immediate terms of Shakespeare's working conditions, while the broadly Marxist approach of Terry Eagleton (*Shakespeare*, 1986) or more narrowly Elliot Krieger's *A Marxist Study of Shakespeare's*

Comedies, 1979, tries to set the plays in a historical frame. A different and more limited kind of historical frame is provided in Norman Blake's *Shakespeare's Language* (1983). It might be added that a more rewarding introduction to Shakespeare's use of language than either Blake's survey of the syntactical and lexical peculiarities or the two books using semiotic techniques is available in Molly Mahood's *Shakespeare's Wordplay* (1957). This small book examining specific passages in the plays for their verbal ingenuity has rightly remained in print when more pretentious works have long vanished.

Poststructuralism and 'deconstructionist' criticism have been applied to Shakespeare in a variety of ways. The most distinct application has taken the concept of 'metatheatre' and found it in all the plays. Metatheatrical elements in Shakespeare's writing are mainly those elements which concern the use of theatre to exemplify the problems of reflexive language. All writers write subjectively, goes the argument, and therefore can write only about the problems of writing, that is, reflexively. Shakespeare's plays use theatre and language to express the inescapable subjectivity of theatrical writing. The 'All the world's a stage' speech from *As You Like It* is an inverted pronouncement about metatheatre, because the stage is the only world there is inside the play. There is no external frame of reference. This concept can even be applied to the sequence of Shakespeare's history plays, which can be read as a progressive analysis which demonstrates the impossibility of writing about anything but the impossibility of using language in the theatre. James L. Calderwood's *Metadrama in Shakespeare's Henriad: 'Richard II' to 'Henry V'* (1979) explores the concept systematically.

Before venturing any distance into the overgrown jungle of theoretical approaches to Shakespeare, many of which use Shakespeare to clarify theory rather than theory to clarify Shakespeare, it may be worth mentioning two critics who use more traditional approaches. They are noteworthy partly because they show some of the durable values of the older approaches, and partly because their unfashionable lack of concern for theory keeps them focused on the plays. They also deal with two of the plays used as examples in this book. Robert Ornstein writes about Shakespeare's history plays in *A Kingdom for a Stage* (1973) from a perspective rooted in nineteenth-century ideas of narrative structure and character psychology, but with a wholly modern freshness. His essay on *1 Henry IV* unashamedly deals with the characters as people, and stands as a brilliant study of Shakespeare as a political analyst of kingship. Antony Brennan's *Shakespeare's Dramatic Structures* (1986) makes use of its author's experience as a stage director and examines how various plays, including *Measure for Measure*, work as stage-plays. In the process it offers a good illustration of how the narrative and poetic qualities inherent in drama can be conjoined in a view of the play as a stage event.

In a fundamental sense all fresh criticism of Shakespeare is likely to take a form which is politically radical. Most of the well-established views are likely to become conservative by process of time, and novelty, whether or not it is announced in explicitly political terms, has to clear its path by rejecting the older views. This is more true of English books like Jonathan Dollimore's *Radical Tragedy* (1984), and the collections of essays such as *Alternative Shakespeares,* ed. John Drakakis (1985), or *Political Shakespeare: new essays in cultural materialism,* edd. Jonathan Dollimore and Alan Sinfield (1985), than of most recent American studies. Many Americans have taken to poststructuralism and deconstruction as a kind of non-political replacement for the New Criticism's art for art's sake approach. J. Hillis Miller and other leading exponents of deconstruction as it can be applied to Shakespeare on the whole provide good examples of using Shakespeare for the sake of the theory instead of the theory for the sake of what it opens in Shakespeare. In America the predominant mode at present is known as the 'New Historicism', and is most strongly represented by Stephen Greenblatt's *Renaissance Self-fashioning: More to Shakespeare* (1980). Its main concern is with the broad cultural context, and the 'subtext' of change and identity which can be traced by this means in the texts. One particularly valuable book using the techniques of this mode is Leonard Tennenhouse's *Power on Display. The Politics of Shakespeare's Genres* (1986).

Much of the freshness of the modern reader-centred approach to Shakespeare comes from its more specialized manifestations, and especially from feminist criticism. The comedies which use role-reversal as the central feature of their plots, so that a boy actor plays a girl playing a boy pretending to be a girl, as Rosalind does in *As You Like It,* offer many opportunities for this kind of approach. Catherine Belsey's *The Subject of Tragedy: Identity and Difference in Renaissance Drama* (1985) despite its title includes a chapter dealing with *As You Like It* and *Twelfth Night*, the central texts for any such discussion. Lisa Jardine, *Still Harping on Daughters: Women and Drama in the Age of Shakespeare* (1983), is entertaining and provocative. Germaine Greer's brief *Shakespeare* (1986), though not specifically feminist, is also thought-provoking.

The Shakespearean tree has many branches, and a host of leaves fall from it every year. Without extending this metaphor beyond its proper scope (which might suggest the thought that fallen leaves are normally gathered up and burned), it can be seen that thinking about Shakespeare criticism as leaves from a deciduous tree has a point. The tree itself lives on after the leaves have fallen. The leaves become a valuable mulch for future growth. The published books and articles about Shakespeare are contributions to an endless variety of discussions which should last as long as the tree itself.

Index

Index